BEST WISHES
GWEN

FLAVOURS OF SPAIN

¶ Libro d guisados
manjares/ y potajes intitulado libro de
cozina: enel qual esta el regimiẽto delas
casas delos reyes y grandes señores: y
los officiales dlas casas dellos cada vno
como an de seruir su officio. ¶ Y enesta
segunda impression se ha añadido vn re-
gimiento delas casas delos caualleros y
gentiles hombres y religiosos de digni-
dades y personas d medianos estados/
y otros que tienen familia & criados en
sus casas: & algũos mãjares de doliẽtes
y otras cosas enel añadidas: todo nue-
uamente reuisto añadido y emendado
por su mismo autor.

¶ Con preuilegio
Imperial.

The title page of the 1529 edition of Rubert de Nola's *Llibre de Coch*, one of the earliest European cookbooks, first published in Barcelona in 1477

FLAVOURS OF SPAIN

A Gastronomic Journey

Jan Read and
Maite Manjón

CASSELL
LONDON

CASSELL LTD.
35 Red Lion Square, London WC1R 4SG
and at Sydney, Auckland, Toronto, Johannesburg,
an affiliate of
Macmillan Publishing Co., Inc.,
New York.

First published 1978

ISBN 0 304 29964 2

Typeset by Inforum Limited, Portsmouth
Printed in Great Britain by
The Camelot Press, Southampton

ACKNOWLEDGEMENTS

All the photographs are by Jan Read except for the Hosteria at Alcalá de Henares and the *horreo* in Galicia, which are reproduced by permission of the Ministerio de Comercio y Turismo. The menu from the Bodega del Riojano in Santander is included by kind permission of the proprietors; and the line engravings are taken from *Recuerdos de un viage por España*, Madrid, 1849, by courtesy of the Hispanic and Luso-Brazilian Council.

Contents

Notes on recipes vii
Introduction 1
Andalusia 11
Levante 30
New Castile 46
Old Castile 65
Aragon and Navarra 79
Catalonia 96
The Balearics 112
The Basque Provinces 127
Asturias and Galicia 142
Extremadura 159
General Index 173
Index of Recipes 176

Illustrations

frontispiece
The title page of Rubert de Nola's *Llibre de Coch*

between pages 54 and 55
The *Tajo* at Ronda
Lamps used for night fishing near Málaga
The former Jewish quarter in Córdoba
A *bodega* in the Levante
Peñiscola, refuge of the last Anti-pope
Cooking a *paella* in the open air

between pages 86 and 87
The *Hostería* at Alcalá de Henares
A typical village in La Mancha
The chalky vineyards of Vega Sicilia, near Valladolid
The winery at Vega Sicilia
A shepherd in the uplands of Aragon

between pages 118 and 119
Chickens grilling outside a restaurant in Barcelona
Son Torrella de Santa María, a Majorcan house
A Majorcan windmill, used for irrigating the land
An outdoor oven for making bread or *coca*
Instrument for removing *cocas* from the oven
Fishing boats in the harbour at Palma, Majorca
Baronial houses at Santillana del Mar near Santander
A *bodega* menu designed by Picasso

between pages 150 and 151
The highly-cured *jamones serranos*
An *horreo* near the Portuguese frontier for storing grain
Trellised vines in Galicia
A peasant in traditional costume near Ciudad Rodrigo
Cooking the evening meal at La Alberca
The Roman Theatre at Mérida

Notes on recipes

Equivalents for cups, glasses and spoons

1 teacup	=	150 ml or 5 fl. oz
1 breakfast cup	=	3 dl or ½ pint
1 liqueur glass	=	30 ml or 1 fl. oz
1 wineglass	=	100 ml or 3 fl. oz
1 teaspoon	=	6 ml or ¼ fl. oz
1 dessertspoon	=	12 ml or ½ fl. oz
1 tablespoon	=	25 ml or 1 fl. oz

These equivalents are approximate.

Flour
Use plain flour unless otherwise stated.

Recipe servings
All recipes serve four people except where otherwise mentioned.

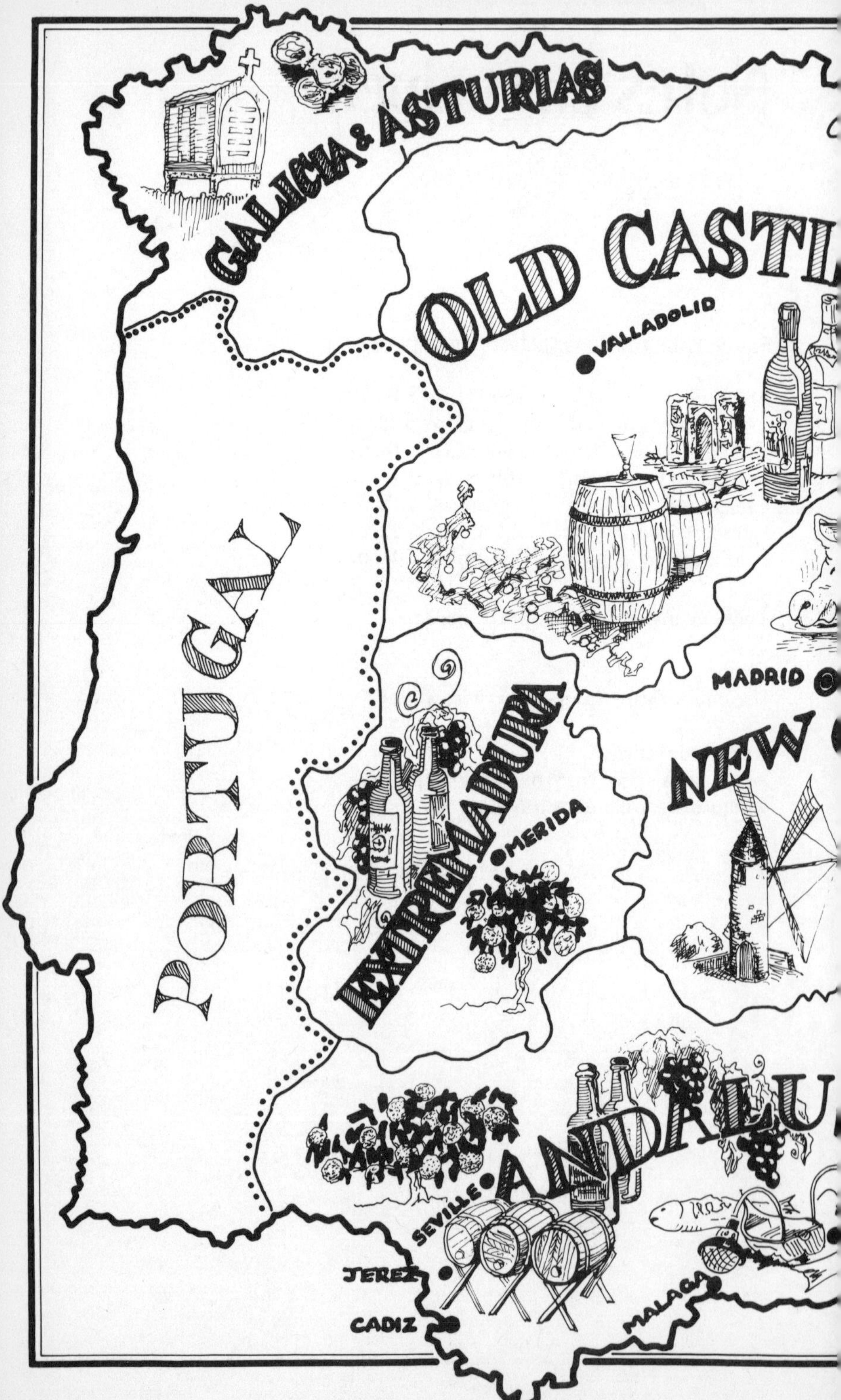
GALICIA & ASTURIAS
OLD CASTI
VALLADOLID
PORTUGAL
EXTREMADURA
MERIDA
MADRID
NEW
ANDALU
SEVILLE
JEREZ
CADIZ
MALAGA

FRANCE
BASQUE PROVINCES
NAVARRA & ARAGON
CATALONIA
BARCELONA
CASTILE
LEVANTE
VALENCIA
MINORCA
MAJORCA
PALMA
THE BALEARICS
IBIZA
FORMENTERA

Con pan y vino
se anda el camino

With bread and wine
The road is short

Introduction

The lively and gastronomic French, who are decidedly the leaders of European civilization in the kitchen, deride the barbarous practices of the Gotho-Iberians, as being darker than Erebus and more ascetic than aesthetic; to credit their authors, a Peninsular breakfast consists of a teaspoonful of chocolate, a dinner, of a knob of garlic soaked in water, and a supper, of a paper cigarette; and according to their *parfait cuisinier*, the *olla* is made of two cigars boiled in three gallons of water – but this is a calumny, a mere invention devised by the enemy . . .

Richard Ford, *Gatherings from Spain*, 1846

The legend that Spanish food is indigestible and limited dies hard. Today it is usually voiced by visitors suffering from 'Mediterranean Tummy', who put down their distressing complaint to food 'swimming in olive oil' – often prepared in seaside hotels in an attempt to provide them with what they are used to at home. But, as Ford, that most urbane and informed of nineteenth-century travellers, adds: 'Genuine and legitimate Spanish dishes are excellent in their way, for no man nor man-cook ever is ridiculous when he does not attempt to be what he is not. The *au naturel* may occasionally be somewhat plain, but seldom makes one sick . . .' To sample the genuine cooking one must fare further afield into the provinces and cities of Spain.

In fact, the Spanish cuisine is as varied and wholesome as any in the world, and it was via Spain that Western Europe received many of the ingredients and recipes that are now its stock in trade. As in France, there was an indigenous style of cookery before the Peninsula became a province of the Roman Empire, but it had little in common with the Mediterranean cooking of today, and the Celt-Iberians made widespread use of animal fats for cooking, particularly from pork.

Among the greatest benefits of Romanization was an improvement in methods of agriculture; apart from a greatly extended cultivation of vines and cereals, the most profound effect on eating habits resulted from their introduction of olive oil and garlic for culinary purposes. This preceded their use in Transalpine Gaul, now southern France, by about a century. The Romans attributed therapeutic properties to garlic – borne out by modern research, which has demonstrated its value in combating thrombosis – and encouraged its consumption by their soldiers and athletes. One of the oldest and best-known Mediterranean sauces, the *alioli* of the Catalans or *aïoli* of Provence, originally made by beating up garlic and olive oil, was a Roman invention, to which Virgil gave the name *moretum*. It later became the practice in Minorca to incorporate eggs in the mixture, and this inspired the *salsa mahonesa*, which took its name from the capital of the island, Port Mahón, and was so much relished by the Duc de Richelieu when he captured the town in 1757 that he introduced it to France as *mayonnaise*.

The second great impact on the Spanish cuisine, as on so many other facets of life in Spain, was that of the Moors. In three short years from Tariq ibn-Ziyad's crossing of the Strait of Gibraltar in 711, the Arabs and their Berber auxiliaries extended the western boundaries of Islam deep into Europe, sweeping through Spain and across the Pyrenees into France. Even today the shadow of the Moors lies heavy across the land. The physical remains are clear to see: the Alhambra at Granada; the Alcázar and Giralda at Seville; the former mosque at Córdoba; the ruined castles silhouetted against the skyline of the sierras; the polychrome tiles, which are such a feature of domestic architecture; and the aqueducts and irrigation works. Culture, manners and language were no less affected; as living testimony, hundreds of Arabic words have passed into other European languages through Spanish, among them *alcohol, algebra, almanac, admiral, syrup, lemon* and *coffee*.

The Moors introduced many new crops and plants to Spain, including spices such as saffron, nutmeg and black pepper. Sugar was was unknown in Western Europe – the common sweetening agent was honey – until they began planting sugar cane in the conquered territories along the Mediterranean coast of the Levante. The bitter orange, lemon and grapefruit were also cultivated in southern Spain some two centuries before the returning Crusaders brought the first specimens to Sicily and Italy from the Near East. The sweet orange came later and was introduced by the Portuguese from China.

Naturally, these new ingredients and flavours had a marked effect on cooking. Possibly because of a shortage of fuel in their North African homelands, the Moors' favourite method of cooking was stewing rather than frying, and the *olla*, a meat and vegetable stew resembling the French *pot au feu*, was the prototype of the many *pucheros, cocidos* and *ranchos* now cooked all over Spain. A favourite ingredient was, and still is, the *garbanzo* or chick-pea, introduced much earlier by the Carthaginians and a source of merriment to Plautus and other writers after him. Alexandre Dumas, who found so little to please him when he made a gastronomic tour of the country in the nineteenth century, wrote of it that 'The *garbanzo* which can be cooked in half-an-hour is without price, but those grown in the barren soil of Spain can be cooked for a year and only become harder – hence the name "musket ball".'

Another Arabic survival is the cold soup or *gazpacho* so popular in Andalusia; and the small cakes and sweetmeats, made in such bewildering profusion in regions formerly occupied by the Moors, often with a basis of ground almonds and egg yolks, reflect their widespread planting of almond groves. After the Reconquest, the Moorish sweetmeats were, ironically enough, perfected and sold by the nuns; and to this day their sale constitutes a valuable source of revenue to the religious orders.

Despite this abundance of confectionery, even now there are few sweets or puddings as they are understood abroad. Flan and baked caramel custard are the great standbys; but the Spanish usually finish a meal with cheese or fresh fruit in season.

During the Middle Ages, when the long centuries of isolation drew to an end with the downfall of the Córdoban caliphate and the inroads of the Christians into al-Andalus, Spanish cuisine became renowned as the richest and most complete in Europe, and its influence was felt as far afield as Sicily and Naples, which formed part of the Crown of Aragon. Nearer home, the Counts of Barcelona dominated the whole of the Languedoc and Provence for a period of some century-and-a-half from 1113. Both regions possessed a common Roman heritage, and the Pyrenees were no barrier to the interchange and sharing of culture. This applied as much to culinary matters as to language and troubadour poetry; and it is far from clear whether many specialities now accepted as Provençal originated east or west of the Pyrenees. *Alioli* (*aïoli*) was a mainstay of Catalan cooking as early as 1024; and there is good reason for supposing that the most famous of fish stews, *bouillabaisse* or *bullabesa* in its Spanish form, was introduced to southern France from Catalonia. The word simply means '*hierve bajo*' or '*bouillir bas*' – 'to boil slowly' – and in both forms the name is a corruption of the original and very similar Catalan or Languedoc.

A most important event in the history of Spanish cooking was the publication in 1477 of the *Llibre de Coch* ('Book of Cookery') in Barcelona. Its author, a Maestre Rubert de Nola, was reputedly chef to Alfonso the Magnanimous of Aragon-Catalonia (1416-58) and accompanied him on the expedition which led to the conquest of Naples. The book was originally written in Catalan, but was revised and translated into Castilian on the initiative of that great gourmand, the Emperor Charles V of Spain. It subsequently ran to some twenty editions – and circulated very widely outside Spain. It is one of the earliest compilations of recipes dating from the mediaeval period; of very considerable variety and sophistication, they ran to 243 in the Castilian edition. Maestre Rubert also includes detailed instructions for the carving of meat and game and the serving of food and drink. He adds some pithy remarks on the functions of the different household officials:

> There are three officials in noble houses, who are never at peace: the carver, the steward and the chef. If the steward brings the meat without properly breaking the bones or provides meat of poor quality, the chef says that he does not know how to buy and that he is a poor steward, and at times they quarrel. Similarly the carver tells the chef that his food is uneatable and that he has no talent for cooking, because the meat is overdone and impossible to carve, with the result that the master loses patience and it is he who is blamed for it. This is the reason why these three officials are never at peace; and if they are to settle their differences among themselves, it is essential that the steward is a good cook and carver, that the chef is a good carver as well as cook, and that the carver is a good steward and chef . . .

After the discovery of the New World by Christopher Columbus in 1492 Spanish cooking still further increased in scope. The explorers and the Conquistadors, such as Cortés and Pizarro, who succeeded him, brought back a wealth of new plants for culinary purposes. The kitchens of France and Western Europe remained innocent of such present-day staples as potatoes, tomatoes, pimientos and chocolate until they were acclimatized and grown in Spain. For example, potatoes were first grown in Europe in the area around Málaga at the suggestion of the Catholic Monarchs, Ferdinand and Isabel.

The pages of *Don Quixote* are evidence enough of the abundance of fare in sixteenth-century La Mancha; and such were the mountains of delicacies provided at the wedding of the rich Camacho that upwards of fifty cooks were required to prepare them. Writing rather earlier, the Chronicler of the Monastery of Guadalupe, the especial shrine of the Conquistadors, lists the New Year farings given to Philip II and D. Sebastián of Portugal in 1587. Philip II's gifts alone included six beautiful doe, three large deer, two wild boar, a hundred partridge, a hundred fowl, two hundred rabbits, a hundred ring doves, four dozen hams, an *arroba* (25 lb) of lard, a hundred bunches of large grapes, an *arroba* of the best candied lemon peel, two *arrobas* of assorted confectionery, six baskets of pippins and another six of apples, and six skins of wine from Ciudad Real.

Depreciation of the Spanish cuisine at the expense of the French began during the seventeenth century at the very time when French cooks were borrowing heavily from Spain and making use of the new colonial products introduced from Spanish America. Thus, María Teresa of Austria, daughter of Philip IV of Spain, who married Louis XIV in 1660, was laughed to scorn at Versailles for her black teeth, attributed to her predilection for chocolate, then unknown in France. A further and special object of attack was her Spanish serving-maid, 'La Molina', who, in the words of Mlle de Montpensier's *Mémoires*, 'assuaged the hunger of her poor mistress by giving her cold pasties, prepared with minced meat, highly seasoned and enveloped in *feuilleté* pastry'. This pastry, which La Grande Mademoiselle goes on to denigrate, was in fact none other than *hojaldre*, the original puff pastry, invented in Spain and for which the French painter Claude Gelée was later eager to take the credit.

In Spain itself a thoroughgoing feeling of inferiority about the national cuisine appears to have spread downwards from the aristocratic court circle of the first of the Spanish Bourbons, Philip V, who left France in 1700 to be crowned King of Spain and whose position was finally regularized after the bitterly contested War of the Spanish Succession. Ordinary Spaniards were far from accepting these strictures; and in Madrid, at any rate, two styles of cookery prevailed: the would-be French of the court and better-to-do, and the traditional of the rest of the population. There are echoes of this controversy in Richard Ford's *Gatherings from Spain*, when, for example, he describes how 'a clever French *artiste* converts an old shoe into an *épigramme d'agneau*, or a Parisian milliner dresses up two deal boards into a fine live *Madame* . . .' But Ford was a traveller who ranged the length and breadth of the country on mule-back and, though he could be scathing in the extreme, knew and loved Spain and never fell into the error of picaresque writers such as Lesage. To judge from a book such as *Gil Blas*, Spain was a barren wilderness inhabited by boorish and ignorant peasants; and foreign views of its poverty and the frugality of its cuisine were reinforced by accounts brought back by the French and British soldiers who fought in the Peninsular War and were operating in a country ravished by the French armies and denuded of supplies.

The French invaders nevertheless paid passing tribute to the survivals of a highly developed cuisine. When General Junot sacked the Monastery of Alcántara near the Portuguese border in 1807 and ordered its mediaeval manuscripts to be used for making cartridges, one of the precious parchments which he preserved and sent to his wife, the Duchess of Abrantes, was the monastery's recipe book. The Duchess later reproduced parts of it in her *Mémoires*, and the famous Escoffier was later to comment that 'It was the major trophy, the only positive advantage which France reaped from that war'. The remark was justified, because the centuries-old manuscript contained the first known references to *consommé* (under the names of '*consumado*' or '*consumo*'), early directions for the use of truffles, and a recipe for *pâté de foie gras*.

Apart from María Teresa of Austria, another Spanish princess has left her mark on the classical French cuisine – but how many people know that when they order a dish with the name '*à l'Empératrice*' or 'Eugénie', that the empress in question was Eugenia de Montijo and that the recipe hails from her native Andalusia? The spirited and pleasure-loving Eugenia, who in 1853 married Louis Philippe, the founder of the short-lived Second Empire, brought to the Tuileries vivid memories of dishes she had enjoyed in Granada during her childhood, of which perhaps the most famous is the fruit compôte known as *riz à l'Empératrice*.

The long and uphill task of reviving pride in the native cuisine and of describing its manifold variety was begun in 1885, when Mariano Pardo de Figueroa and José Castro y Serrano published a book under the pseudonyms of *El doctor Thebussem y Un cocinero de S.M.* (Dr Thebussem and a Cook of Your Majesty). In their introduction they wrote that 'Spanish cooking today stands in need of writers to revive its traditions and uncover its glorious past, so as to make available its methods and achievements to the whole of society from cook to king'. The immediate outcome was a rash of cookbooks, written in haste and without knowledge, which indiscriminately mixed Spanish recipes with others from abroad, copied from earlier books. It was only during the first decades of the present century that skilled and informed chefs, such as Ignacio

Doménech and Teodoro Bardají, produced large compilations of genuine Spanish recipes and that Dionisio Pérez published his now classical *Guia del buen comer español.* It is on sources such as these and, of course, on traditions of regional cooking which have survived intact, that the present book is based.

The history of Spanish wines is as long and honourable as that of its cuisine. The vine was probably indigenous, but all the invaders of classical times - the Phoenicians, the Greeks and the Carthaginians – improved on the wild varieties by processes of selection, in all likelihood brought strains from abroad and introduced new and better methods of making wine. Great strides were made during the period of Roman occupation, when, between the requirements of the colonists, the new urban population and the ever-thirsty legionaries, there was a greatly increased demand. Production had so far increased by the beginning of the first century that wine was being exported to Rome from the Peninsula, and to protect the Italian growers strict limitations were enforced on the planting of new vineyards in the Hispanic provinces. The sweet wines of Málaga were a great favourite at the time and they were praised not only by the Spanish-born Columella, but by Pliny, Democritus and Virgil. The large earthenware vessels, so similar in shape to the Roman amphorae, and still in use in the region of Montilla, near Córdoba, and at Valdepeñas in La Mancha, are a direct survival from this period.

The Moors were forbidden the consumption of wine by the Koran, but many Moorish poems testify to its pleasures, so that al-Mu'tamid, the poet king of Seville, could write:

As I was passing by
A vine, its tendrils tugged my sleeve.
'Do you design,' said I,
'My body so to grieve?'
'Why do you pass,' the vine
Replied, 'and never greeting make?
It took this blood of mine
Your thirsting bones to slake.'*

Spain is a country first and foremost famous for one wine, sherry, and the wines from Jerez were well-liked by the Romans. They were being exported to England as early as 1340 during the reign of Edward III, and Chaucer, good vintner's son as he was, warns his reader that 'there riseth such fumositee' from the wines of near-by

*Translated by A.J. Arberry, *Moorish Poetry*, Cambridge, 1953.

Lepe that he might well imagine himself to be in Spain rather than at his tavern in Cheapside. The English trade received a great fillip after the capture of Granada in 1492, when the Catholic Monarchs expelled the Jews, among them the merchants of Jerez, and many English traders settled there in their place. They faced recurrent difficulties in face of the hostility between the two countries in Tudor times, but an unexpected outcome of Sir Francis Drake's raid on Cadiz in 1587, when he seized 2900 pipes of wine, was simply to clinch its popularity at home.

Under their old name of sack (probably from the Spanish *sacar*, to 'export'), the wines, which were much sweeter than modern sherries, were a prime favourite with the Elizabethans. They lost out to port during the eighteenth century, when the Methuen Treaty of 1703 was signed to stimulate commerce between England and Portugal at the expense of wines from elsewhere; but the trade picked up during the late 1700s, and there was a further boom after the Peninsular War. Most of the great sherry dynasties date from this period, many of them founded by English, Scottish and Irish merchants who settled in the area to supervise the making and shipping of the wine. Their names survive in those of the great sherry firms of today, such as Duff Gordon, Osborne, Garvey, Gonzalez Byass, Sandeman or Williams and Humbert, although most are now Spanish-owned.

Of the other Spanish wines traditionally drunk in England, the best-known were Málaga and Tarragona, but both have suffered something of an eclipse. Málaga was once described by André Simon as 'the perfect "Ladies' Wine" in Victorian days'; it is still a splendid dessert wine, but has suffered from the current vogue for dry wines. The Tarragona so popular in Victorian pubs was a rough red wine, sweetened and fortified in imitation of port. Centuries earlier Catalonia had been making choice table wines, as it does today; and in the shadow of the viaduct at Montserrat, near Barcelona, there are vineyards first planted in Roman times.

Except in the high sierras, almost every region of Spain, apart from the far north and north-west, produces table wines, ranging from the *vinos valientes* of Murcia, inky black in colour and sometimes containing more alcohol than a light sherry, to the pale and flowery *vinos verdes* of Galicia, with their elusive sparkle on the tongue.

Among the best-known and most carefully made of these table wines are those from the Rioja, an upland district lying along the valley of the River Ebro on the borders of Navarra and Old Castile. It, too, has a long history of wine-making, dating from Phoenician and Roman times, if not earlier.

The Moors called this region of grapes and wines '*Veled Assikia*' and it was one of the first to be liberated during the Christian Reconquest. Its vineyards were much expanded to meet a brisk demand for the wines by the Conquistadors in the Americas. Increased production was sometimes achieved at the expense of quality, and during the seventeenth and eighteenth centuries a series of regulations, municipal and regional, were imposed to maintain and improve standards. It was nevertheless partly as a result of the disaster that struck the vineyards of Bordeaux that the Rioja became recognized as a major producer of fine wines.

From 1875 that insect pest of the vine, phylloxera, wreaked havoc with the vines in Bordeaux. It was later to spread to the Rioja in 1905, but in the interim period, while a solution was being found in grafting native vines on to resistant American stocks, supplies were made good from the Rioja. There had already been liaison between growers in the two areas – to the benefit of the Spanish wines – but French viticulturalists now settled in the Rioja, either buying vineyards or to supervise and improve production, and from this time the Rioja wines were increasingly made by Bordeaux methods.

In terms of climate and geography Spain is a country of contrasts. It is difficult to imagine greater extremes than the green hills and fertile pastures of the Basque country and Atlantic coast; the endless grey-green olive groves of Seville and Jaén; the paddyfields and orange groves of Valencia; the semi-tropical *vega* of Granada; the vast wheatfields and vineyards of La Mancha; or the rolling scrubland of the Extremadura with its cork oaks and roving flocks of sheep and pigs. All cooking reflects the availability of local ingredients, and Spain is still a country where the best dishes are those made from such local ingredients as are in season and the best cheap wine is the wine from the neighbourhood. It is true that modern transport and the march of tourism have resulted in much greater flexibility: the visitor asks for and gets his bottle of Rioja, his *gazpacho* and his steak, wherever he may be; but any serious study of Spanish food and wine must be on a regional basis.

The regions described in the book, at one time or another kingdoms in their own right, are convenient divisions not only for gastronomic purposes but also in setting out something of the history and culture of areas, which, late in their history and somewhat insecurely, were welded into a whole.

As regards the practical details of a tour, wherever you start and in whichever direction you head, there are always interesting things to see and good food and wine to sample. One or other of the larger scale 1:1,000,000 Michelin or Firestone sheets is more or less essential in arranging the details. Mention is made of some of the hotels and restaurants which are of special interest and most typical of the different regions; but the book is not a gazetteer, and the most up-to-date and comprehensive list of hotels and restaurants is that of the red *Michelin Guide to Spain and Portugal.*

Spain is fortunate in possessing a chain of some eighty government-run hotels, the Paradores and Albergues, unique in their wide coverage of the country. The Paradores are often installed in carefully restored castles, monasteries and palaces, sometimes dating from mediaeval times and in themselves affording the visitor an insight into the country's history. The Albergues are comfortable stopping places, sited on the main motor routes or, like the Paradores, in the more remote country districts, where ordinary hotel accommodation is not easily available. Both offer comfortable rooms with private bathrooms at very reasonable prices; and the Ministry of Tourism, which controls them, makes a point of serving regional food and wines in their dining-rooms. It also runs restaurants, known as Hosterías, again in the charming surroundings of buildings such as the Colegio Trilingüe of the ancient University of Alcalá de Henares, near Madrid. Culinary standards are not uniform in these establishments and depend very much on the individual management and the resources of the neighbourhood; some of those that are outstanding are mentioned by name.

Spain is a hospitable land; and there is an old custom, dating from Moorish times, that when a Spaniard is at table he will say to a passing acquaintance or even to a stranger, '*Vd. gusta*?' ('Will you join me?') The correct reply is a polite '*Que approveche*' ('May you enjoy it') – which is what we should like to say to the reader embarking on a gastronomic tour.

Andalusia

Andalusia takes its name from al-Andalus, the southern part of Spain occupied for so many centuries by the Moors and extending in the heyday of the Córdoban caliphate from the River Ebro in the north to the Mediterranean and southern Portugal. Modern Andalucía, divided from the Castilian plateau by the rugged heights of the Sierra Morena, which proved such an obstacle to the French during the Peninsular War and to other invaders before them, covers a much smaller, but still very considerable, area in the south of Spain.

It is the part of the country which most visitors think of as typically 'Spanish', with its almond and olive groves, the sherry vineyards, the white houses and patios, the flamenco dancers, the Easter *feria* in Seville and its hooded penitents and processions – and above all the beating sun, which makes a *siesta* more or less obligatory in high summer.

Many of its inhabitants are directly descended from the Moors, and not so long ago it was the custom for the women to go veiled in the seaside villages near Cadiz. There is a tendency to think of the Andalusians as dark-skinned, volatile and lazy, with a perpetual *mañana* on their lips, and to identify them with the *gitanos* of the Sacromonte in Granada; but this of course is to underestimate them. Perhaps more typical of modern Andalusia are the irrigation schemes and the neat new villages built during the Franquist regime, from which men and women alike go out to a hard day's work in the cottonfields or to pick olives or grapes.

Once in the Moorish or Jewish quarter of a city like Córdoba, with the houses built close against the dazzling sun and sometimes thrust apart by pointed arches across the narrow cobbled thoroughfare, time seems to have stood still. Córdoba was the heart of Muslim Spain. After 'Abd-al-Rahman I, exiled from his native Syria, founded the Umayyad emirate in Spain, it was Córdoba that he made his capital in 756, and so it remained until the dynasty came to an end in the early years of the eleventh century, when al-Andalus, split by internal dissension, broke up into the so-called *taifas* or 'party kingdoms' and lay a prey to the advancing Christians from the north.

During this period the mantle of Córdoba descended on nearby Seville; and here the most interesting Moorish relics are the Alcázar (or royal palace), with its splendid polychrome tiles and shaded gardens, and the Giralda, once the minaret of the mosque, which flanks the great Gothic cathedral. A reminder that Seville, which stands on the River Guadalquivir, was later the centre for the colonial trade with Spanish America, is the foursquare Renaissance building housing the Archives of the Indies; and the suburb of Triana is famous both for its gypsies and for being the venue of the Easter processions.

Sightseeing in Seville is hot and thirsty work, and when you have seen enough, make your way to the Calle de las Sierpes in the centre. It is closed to traffic and cool even in summer thanks to the overhead awnings stretched between the housetops. Sit down at one of the tables in the street, with its inviting white tablecloth, outside any of its numerous restaurants; order a glass of chilled montilla; look at the menu and ask for *ensalada sevillana* (page 22) or *huevos a la flamenca* (page 25) – and then if you are wise, order more montilla to drink through the meal, as the Sevillanos do themselves . . .

Two other great cities of Andalusia, Málaga and Granada, are closely linked with the Moors, and both lie in the former Kingdom of Granada to the south-east. When the caliphate broke up, Granada was not the largest of the small Moorish principalities formed from the ruins, but it was to prove the longest-lived, and it was not until Castile and Aragon were united under the Catholic Monarchs that the Christians moved in for the kill. First to fall was Málaga in 1487. The ruins of the great castle of Djabal Faro ('the hill of light', so-called because of its great beacon), where the Moors made their fierce last stand, lies close to the modern Parador of Gibralfaro, and you may look across at its jagged silhouette while enjoying the *ajo blanco de Málaga* (page 20) and others of its regional specialities on the wide terrace, which also overlooks the blue waters of the bay.

The centre now of the flourishing tourist region of the Costa del Sol, Málaga, bustling and cheerful as it is, is not particularly rich in historic buildings, but you may well care to visit the old-fashioned bars in the centre, where Málaga wines in all their variety are served from the wood. The most poetic description of an old Málaga is perhaps that of Harry Yoxall, writing in *Wine & Food* magazine: 'There are interesting, almost surprising undertones beneath its unctuous richness, like the dark fires in the heart of a jewel. Just as the touch of something very cold leaves you uncertain whether it has frozen or burnt you, so in the taste of great Málagas the sugar is sublimated and becomes almost astringent.'

By 1491 King Ferdinand had overrun the whole of the Kingdom of Granada except the city itself and established the great tented camp of Santa Fe beneath the walls of the Alhambra. The last of its Moorish sovereigns, the luckless Boabdil, delivered up the keys of the city in January 1492 and rode off into exile, pursued by his mother's ringing epitaph: 'Weep like a woman for what you could not defend like a man.'

Granada itself is now ringed by ugly double carriageways and high-rise buildings, and its somewhat dank streets seem a world apart from the airy phantasies of the Alhambra above. The pleasantest place to stay is at the Parador of San Francisco, actually inside the precinct of the Alhambra and incorporating Moorish arches and plasterwork – but book a long time ahead; accommodation is limited and it is always full. Here you may sample cold soups made with almonds, the famous *tortilla al Sacromonte* (page 26) and a variety of dishes made with the splendid vegetables from the lush *vega* (or garden), where Ferdinand pitched his camp.

Although it is not strictly in Andalusia as it is understood today, but in the neighbouring province of Huelva towards the Portuguese frontier, nobody should visit the south of Spain without seeing the Coto Doñana. This 600,000-acre nature reserve, on the coast between Cadiz and Palos de la Frontera, from where Columbus first sailed for America, is perhaps the most remarkable in Europe. It is situated in the swampy delta of the River Guadalquivir and its marshlands provide a resting place for great flocks of birds on their migrations between Africa and Europe and a more permanent home for wild animals of all sorts, such as red deer, foxes, lynx and eagles. To reach the Coto Doñana you must make a wide detour to the north, since there are no bridges across the Guadalquivir north of Seville, but the southern fringe of the *marismas* (or marshes) may clearly be seen across the estuary at Sanlúcar de Barrameda on the western extreme of the sherry country.

Jerez de la Frontera and the neighbouring city of Cadiz are the high point of any gastronomic tour of Andalusia. From whichever direction you approach, you will drive through rolling country with the vivid green vines marching across its gentle slopes. The landscape, with its chalky white *albariza* soil, on which the best of the grapes, the Palomino, is grown, has an almost lunar aspect. Here and there the *bienteveos*, rough shelters roofed with esparto grass matting, from which armed guards once kept an eye on the ripening crop, are still to be seen; and there is an old proverb in Jerez: *Las niñas y las viñas difíciles son de guardar* ('Girls and vines are difficult to guard').

The old and picturesque custom of treading the grapes with *zapatos de pisar*, cowhide boots studded with flat tacks, and of squeezing out the juice in presses with a large wooden screw is now dying out. The job is now done as effectively and at much less expense in modern presses of German design, in which the grapes are squeezed against the side of a metal cylinder by an inflatable rubber bag. The *bodegas* in Jerez, where the wine is matured and elaborated and which Richard Ford described as resembling 'cathedrals in size and loftiness', survive in the form in which they were built in the late eighteenth and nineteenth centuries. The big sherry concerns welcome visitors and provide guided tours during working hours in the morning (from about 9.30 a.m. until noon).

The heart of any bodega is the *soleras*. Once inside the lofty arcaded interior, the first impression is of mountainous piles of butts awaiting their time in the cool, dark reaches; but the blending and maturing of sherry is a highly complex process. The new wine first undergoes a period of probation in what is aptly called the *criadera* or 'nursery'. A peculiarity of sherry is that no two butts develop in quite the same fashion, and a second entirely individual characteristic is that the wines spontaneously grow a *flor* or 'flower', consisting of a thick wrinkled layer of yeast cells, which protects them from the air. Unlike other wines, which turn into vinegar unless matured out of contact with the atmosphere, they are therefore aged in butts that are only loosely stoppered – a procedure which permits slow and controlled development and results in their entirely individual bouquet and flavour.

After about two years in cask, when the wine has been racked free of suspended solids and sparingly fortified with alcohol, each butt is individually classified according to the type of sherry for which it is best suited and is ready to become part of the *solera* proper. The word comes from the Latin *solum*, or Spanish *suelo*, meaning a 'floor'; and the butts are arranged in 'scales', each consisting of long rows of butts containing wine of similar age and type. The procedure is to draw off wine for blending and shipping from the butts first laid down, which are then topped up or 'refreshed' with rather less mature wine, and so on down all the five or more 'scales' of the *solera* to the youngest wine from the *criadera*. This continuous blending of younger with older wine makes it possible to reproduce the flavour and style of a well-known branded sherry such as La Ina or Tio Pepe from year to year with very little difference.

The routine of a visit has apparently changed very little from Ford's time:

> Here the swarthy professor, dressed somewhat like Figaro in the *Barber of Seville*, is followed by sundry jacketed and sandalled Ganymedes, who bear glasses on waiters; the lecturer is armed with a long stick, to the end of which is tied a bit of hollow cane, which he dips in each butt; the subject is begun at the beginning, and each step in advance is explained to the listening party with the gravity of a judicious foreman of a jury: the sample is handed round and tasted by all, who, if they are wise, will follow the example of their leader (on whom wine has no more effect than on a glass), by never swallowing the sips, but only permitting the tongue to agitate it in the mouth . . .

Although garb has changed and the *venencia* has evolved into an elegant silver cup mounted on a whalebone stem, the essentials are the same.

Nowadays the tasting usually takes place in a comfortable bar, and, drunk fresh and on the spot – *finos* are, for example, served as they properly should be, chilled and from half-bottles – the wines are of truly remarkable flavour and bouquet. Apart from the dry and delicate *finos*, the other main types are *amontillado*, a deeper coloured wine with a full 'nutty' flavour, and *oloroso*. This is a darker style of sherry than the others; in its natural state it is completely dry, but it is often blended with a sweet must made from the Pedro Ximénez grape to make dessert sherries, of which one of the best-known examples is Bristol Cream. The light and aromatic *manzanilla fina* is not made in Jerez de la Frontera, but in Sanlúcar de Barrameda, some twenty kilometres to the west. The drive through the vineyards is very pleasant, and quite the best way of drinking *manzanilla* is at one of the shellfish bars overlooking the river at Sanlúcar.

Sherry is not the only good wine made in Andalusia. Apart from the sweet dessert wines of Málaga (see page 8), the hilly region of Montilla-Moriles south of Córdoba makes wines very similar in style to sherry, and until fairly recently much of it in fact went to Jerez for blending. If you are driving from Córdoba to Málaga, the picturesque little town of Montilla, the Munda Betica of the Romans and the scene of fierce fighting when Julius Caesar destroyed the rump of Pompey's armies, is well worth a visit. In its numerous bodegas they make wine not in butts as in Jerez, but in large earthenware *tinajas* reminiscent of Roman amphorae. Montilla grows a *flor* like sherry, but is strong enough in alcohol not to be fortified. Dry, light and aromatic, it is a favourite apéritif and is frequently drunk all through the meal. This is also true of *fino* sherries in the Jerez region – wines made for local consumption do not undergo the slight additional fortification of those for export and are therefore less 'heady'.

A short distance to the south of Jerez, by way of Puerto de Sta María, also a centre for making sherry and Spanish brandy, and across a narrow causeway, lies the glittering sea-girt city of Cadiz, in many respects the gastronomic capital of Andalusia. It is a place which has often been destroyed and rebuilt and was founded by the Phoenicians near the legendary Tartessos of the ancient world. After a period of decline during the mediaeval period it came into prominence again as a main centre for the seaborne trade with Spanish America. Its present elegant white houses and domed churches date from 1596, when the place was razed to the ground during the destructive raid by the English under the Earl of Essex. Later, during the Peninsular War, Cadiz remained one of the few islands of Spanish resistance; and in 1812 the Cadiz Cortes (parliament) framed the liberal constitution, which was a model of its kind of Europe.

On gastronomic maps of Spain, Andalusia is often labelled the *Zona de los fritos* or 'region of fried food', and high on the list of such dishes must come the fries of mixed fish (see page 24), often called *parejas* in Cadiz – this being the name of the dish cooked by the fishermen while at sea in their boats. The Atlantic coast is exceptionally rich in fish, particularly tuna, sardines, *chocos* (a variety of inkfish), the gleaming silver scabbard fish, the ugly but delicious '*perros*' and '*gatos*' ('dogs' and 'cats') akin to the whiting (see recipe, page 24), and the shad, such a favourite of the Moors, which swims up the rivers in the spring. Shellfish, too, is abundant and was plentiful and cheap until modern methods of refrigeration and transport led to its shipment to markets further afield. A local speciality is the *ostion*, somewhat similar to the Portuguese oyster, not eaten on its own, but used to give flavour and piguancy to the famous *sopa al cuarto de hora* (page 21).

Not so long ago some of the fish was caught by allowing it to swim into *caños* or pools, which were then dammed up. During the year the salinity of the water increased because of evaporation, and when the fish had grown and multiplied the pool was emptied and the owner and his friends gathered to scoop them out by hand. Their long sojourn in the salty water gave them an especially good flavour. A somewhat similar custom prevailed along the shores of Huelva, where the fish pools were the perquisite of the Dukes of Osuna.

Cadiz is perhaps the original home of the fish and chip shop, in the form of its *freidurías*, of which the famous Dr Thebussem wrote almost a century ago:

> Fish from the *freidor* is unbeatable: it is as different from that prepared by chefs or cooks as the wine of Jerez from other wines, the sword from Toledo from other swords, and the olives from Seville from other olives. Because of the special and secret method of cutting the fish and the temperature of the oil, the aroma rising from the sole, mullet, whiting, sardines and other fish cooking in the steaming olive oil is an invitation to eat; and few suppers are more agreeable than this fried fish, washed down by half-a-dozen glasses of aromatic manzanilla.

Málaga, too, is famous for its fish and its fishermen, whose boats, as described by Lorca in his *Canto Nocturno*, still stand out to sea, their lights ranged like lamp-posts on the night horizon:

Ay muchacha, muchacha
cuanto barco en el puerto de Málaga.

Characteristic of these Mediterranean waters are the *boquerones* (fresh anchovies) and *chanquetes* (a form of whitebait), also at their best when fried crisp and served with slices of lemon.

Perhaps the best-known of Andalusia's contributions to cooking are its cold soups or *gazpachos* (pages 19 and 20). These always contain garlic and a little olive oil and vinegar, but may be made with a variety of uncooked vegetables, chopped or purééd. A popular version contains peppers, tomatoes and cucumber, but on no account miss the *ajo blanco de Málaga* with its whole fresh grapes or the *sopa de almendras* from Granada, made with a basis of ground almonds. During the winter the Andalusians also make a hot *gazpacho* (page 20).

A region as extensive and as fertile as Andalusia has a great variety of regional dishes, some of which are described in the recipe section that follows, and it is possible to mention only a few of them.

Salads, such as the *ensalada sevillana* (page 22), are always good; one of the most intriguing is the *remojón*, containing onion, garlic and flaked *bacalao* (dried and salted cod) with a little orange to give it edge and piquancy.

A perennial favourite from Seville and a supper dish easily made at home is *huevos a la flamenca* (page 25), consisting of eggs fried in a sauce made from onions and tomatoes and garnished with prawns, the spicy *chorizo* sausage and strips of red pepper. The gypsy-inspired *tortilla al Sacromonte* is a substantial variation on the Spanish omelette; and other main courses popular in the area are *menudo gitano*, prepared from chicken giblets and other ingredients, and *callos a la andaluza*, somewhat similar to the piquant *callos a la madrileña* (Madrid-style tripe), but made with the addition of chick-peas. A good place to try typical dishes like these is the excellent restaurant of the small Albergue at Antequera, which also serves a most appetizing fish pie made of different types of white fish, flaked and mixed with onion and grated carrot beaten up with eggs, then cooked and served with a lobster sauce.

There are two first-rate hams from the region, cured in the style of *jamón serrano* (page 161); and indeed Jabugo disputes with Montánchez in the Extremadura the claim for making the best cured ham of this sort – rather similar to those from Bayonne and Parma – in the whole of Spain. The other comes from the small village of Trevélez in the Alpujarras mountains east of Granada, the last stronghold of the Moors after the fall of the city to the Christians.

Last but not least is the multiplicity of cakes and sweetmeats in the Moorish tradition, best bought in the *confiterías* or confectionaries. Among the best-known are the *yemas de San Leandro*, reputedly made by dripping strands of egg yolk from a small inverted and perforated cone into hot syrup – but the secret remains with the nuns. Another confection from Seville is *membrillo*, the quince compôte or paste, which was such a favourite of Pedro de Luna, the last of the Antipopes; it was by dosing it with arsenic that his enemies made an unsuccessful attempt to kill him. The custom in Andalusia is to take sherry with a powdery sweetmeat wrapped in twists of paper, and these *polvorones* (recipe, page 29) are manufactured in Estepona on the main road from Córdoba to Málaga. The whole town is fragrant with the aroma of hot sugar and almonds, and if you stop off at one of the manufacturies to sample their wares, they will serve the sherry free.

Recipes

SALSA A LA ANDALUZA
ANDALUSIAN SAUCE

A piquant variation on mayonnaise. The following ingredients are stirred into ordinary mayonnaise (see page 116). The amounts will depend on the quantity of sauce which you require, but the garnish should be used sparingly.

A little tomato purée
Finely chopped red pimiento
Chopped parsley
Lemon juice

GAZPACHO ANDALUZ
GAZPACHO ANDALUSIAN STYLE

5 oz (150 g) fresh breadcrumbs
4 large ripe tomatoes, blanched, peeled and chopped
½ cucumber, chopped small
4 green peppers, chopped very fine
4 tablespoons olive oil
Salt and pepper
2 cloves garlic, peeled
3 tablespoons vinegar

Put the fresh breadcrumbs, chopped tomatoes, cucumber and green peppers and olive oil into a large bowl. Stir with 1¾ pints (1 litre) of water and leave for 1 hour to soak. Rub the mixture through a sieve or put it into a blender so as to make a purée, adding salt and pepper to taste. Grind the garlic in a mortar, stir with the vinegar and transfer to the bowl.

If desired, some of the cut-up green pepper and cucumber may be reserved and served on the side. The soup must be served well chilled and should be put in the refrigerator, but covered with foil or a tight-fitting lid to prevent the flavour spreading.

Gazpacho caliente gaditano
Hot gazpacho from Cadiz

Gazpacho is not always served cold, and this version is a favourite in Andalusia during the winter.

1 lb (½ kg) tomatoes
4 cloves garlic
1 green pepper, cut up small
4 tablespoons refined olive oil
1 teaspoon salt
1¼ pints (¾ litre) water, from cooking the tomatoes
2 oz (60 g) fresh brown breadcrumbs
½ teaspoon sweet paprika powder

Boil the tomatoes in the stated amount of water for ten minutes. Pour off and reserve the water, cover the tomatoes with cold water, remove the skins and put the blanched tomatoes on a plate. Grind the garlic and green pepper in a large mortar or bowl, then add the blanched tomatoes, olive oil and salt. Make a purée of the mixture by rubbing it through a sieve or putting it into a blender and adding the breadcrumbs, together with the sweet paprika and half of the reserved water. Now transfer to a soup dish, stir until thoroughly mixed and pour in the rest of the water at the boil. Serve very hot.

Ajo blanco con uvas de Malaga
Cold garlic soup with grapes

20 almonds or an equal amount of pine kernels
2 cloves garlic
1 teaspoonful salt
2 oz (60 g) stale breadcrumbs, soaked and drained
4 tablespoons olive oil
2 tablespoons vinegar
½ lb (225 g) white grapes, skinned and without pips

Blanch the almonds in boiling water and skin them. Leave for a few minutes to cool, then grind them in a mortar or use a 'Mouli' parsley mincer if you find it easier. Put the ground almonds in a bowl, together with the crushed garlic, salt and moist breadcrumbs. Drip in the olive oil little by little, stirring with a wooden spoon as if making a mayonnaise, add the vinegar, and when the mixture is smooth and creamy stir in 25 fl. oz (¾ litre) of water. Cover with a lid or foil and leave in the refrigerator until well chilled. Add the grapes just before serving.

Sopa de almendras de Ronda
Almond soup from Ronda

A hot almond soup from the mountain town of Ronda.

14 oz (400 g) roasted almonds
2 oz (60 g) caster sugar
1 stick cinnamon
Peel of 1 lemon, in a single piece
1 oz (30 g) bread, cut up small

Grind the almonds in a mortar with the sugar or use a 'Mouli' mincer if you prefer. Add to a saucepan containing 1¾ pints (1 litre) of water, together with the cinnamon and lemon peel. Bring the water to the boil and simmer for 5 minutes, then add the bread and cook for another 10 minutes until the bread has disintegrated and the liquid is smooth. Remove the lemon peel and serve very hot.

Sopa al cuarto de hora
Quarter-of-an-hour soup

So-called because of the cooking time, it is at its best when made with *ostiones* (see page 16), but clams are a satisfactory alternative.

4 tablespoons olive oil
1 small onion, chopped
2 cloves garlic, peeled and chopped
3½ oz (100 g) bread, thinly sliced
2 oz (60 g) cooked ham, diced
2½ pints (1½ litres) water
Salt
16 clams, cooked and removed from the shell
1 hard-boiled egg, chopped
1 small glass dry sherry
Chopped parsley

Heat a little olive oil in a large saucepan, fry the onion for a few minutes, then add the garlic, bread, ham and water, and season with salt. Simmer for ¼ hour and shortly before removing from the fire, add the clams, chopped hard-boiled egg and sherry. Sprinkle with parsley and serve hot.

Ensalada sevillana
Seville salad

Salad

3 oz (100 g) rice, boiled and drained
3 canned red peppers, cut into strips
6 spring onions
4 tomatoes, sliced
7 oz (200 g) Seville olives, without stones

Heap the rice in the middle of a serving dish, arrange the other ingredients decoratively around it, and then pour on the following vinaigrette sauce:

Vinaigrette sauce

1 clove garlic
2 tablespoons vinegar
4 tablespoons refined olive oil
Salt and pepper
Chopped parsley

Crush the garlic into a cup, add the other ingredients and beat well with a spoon until emulsified. After pouring the sauce over the salad, it should be garnished with a little chopped parsley.

Salsa de patata para pescado
Potato sauce for fish

This is served with any fried, baked or boiled white fish.

½ lb (225 g) potatoes
Olive oil
2 red peppers, fresh or canned and cut into strips
10 oz (300 g) tomatoes, blanched and peeled
Salt
A few cumin seeds
1 bay leaf

If the peppers are fresh they must be fried very slowly for 1 hour with a minute amount of olive oil and turned at intervals. Skin them, remove and discard pips and capsules, and cut them into strips.

Peel the potatoes, cut them up and fry them in hot olive oil until golden. Drain off excess oil, add the peppers and tomatoes and cook for another 10 minutes. Now add the salt, cumin seeds and bay leaf, together with a breakfast cup of water or a little more if necessary, and simmer for 5 minutes more. Finally rub the mixture through a fine sieve.

GAMBAS FRITAS
FRIED PRAWNS

1 lb (450 g) prawns in shell
2 cloves garlic, crushed
1 tablespoon chopped parsley
1 tablespoon olive oil

Boil the prawns for 5 minutes, if the fishmonger has not already done this; otherwise they need simply be washed and drained.

Heat the olive oil in a pan, add the prawns and garlic and fry for 10 minutes, turning the prawns so that they cook on both sides. Stir in the parsley and serve immediately while they are still sizzling hot.

They must be peeled at the table, so fingerbowls should be provided.

LOS FIELES MUSULMANES ORANDO EN EL MIHRAB.

Fritos variados de pescados a la Andaluza
Mixed fried fish Andalusian style

2 small whiting, cut into pieces
2 small sole
2 small flounder or plaice
2 inkfish (squid), cleaned and cut into rings
½ lb (225 g) *boquerones* (fresh anchovies)
7 oz (200 g) whitebait
Flour
Salt
Olive oil

This mixed fry may be made from whatever white fish are available, provided they are small – the bigger the variety, the more contrasting the flavours and the better the result. Larger fish may also be used by cutting them into pieces.

Inkfish, if available, lend the dish a particularly good flavour, as they do to *paella* – do not be put off by their appearance. Choose them small or medium-sized and to clean them, first pull away the body from the head and tentacles. Cut the tentacles from the head (they are the most tender part of the fish) and discard the rest of it together with the attached gut. Pull the flat spine from the body and strip away the thin outer membrane. Wash the body well, then turn it inside out and wash again before cutting it into rings, when it is ready for dredging and cooking.

The other fish should also be cleaned, washed and dried. Season with salt, dredge in flour and fry briskly in batches until browned. Blot off excess oil on kitchen paper and serve immediately with wedges of lemon.

Caldillo de perro

The name is untranslatable. It is a rich soup containing slices of fish known colloquially in Andalusia as 'dogs'. The nearest English equivalent is whiting.

1 whiting of about 2 lb (1 kg)
Salt
Olive oil
2 cloves garlic
1 onion, chopped fine
Juice of 1 orange (use bitter orange when available)

Clean, wash and dry the fish, then cut it into slices about 2 inches (5 cm) thick, sprinkle with salt and leave on a plate for 1 hour.

Heat a little olive oil in a pan, fry the cloves of garlic until golden, then remove and discard them. Add the chopped onion and cook for 2 or 3 minutes, then pour in 1¾ pints (1 litre) of water, add the pieces of fish and boil slowly for some 15 minutes. Finally, add the orange juice and serve piping hot.

HUEVOS A LA FLAMENCA
EGGS FLAMENCA

In Spain, this dish, so typical of Seville, is always cooked and served straight from the fire in individual earthenware *cazuelas* (see page 32).

Olive oil
4 small onions, sliced
8 oz (225 g) green bacon, chopped
4 or 5 tomatoes, peeled and sliced
Salt and pepper
8 oz (225 g) *chorizo* (see page 161), thinly sliced
1 or 2 eggs per person
1 medium-sized can red peppers, cut into strips
8 oz (225 g) peeled prawns (fresh or frozen and defrosted)

Heat a little olive oil in a pan and fry the onions until tender, then drain off the oil. Add the chopped bacon and sliced tomatoes, fry for another 5 or 10 minutes and season with salt and pepper. Remove the mixture with a draining spoon and divide it between four small *cazuelas* or fireproof dishes. Arrange the *chorizo* around the edge of the dishes, break the eggs in the middle and cook over a medium flame until the whites are set, the yolks remaining soft. Place the prawns and strips of red pepper decoratively over the top and serve at once.

Tortilla al Sacromonte
Omelette Sacromonte

So-called because it hails from the gypsy quarter of Granada.

2 lamb's brains
2 lamb's sweetbreads
Salt and pepper
8 eggs
Toasted breadcrumbs
Olive oil
3 medium-sized potatoes, peeled and diced
2 red peppers, deseeded and diced

Wash the brains and sweetbreads thoroughly in cold water so as to remove all traces of blood. Rinse them in fresh water, remove the membranes from the brains, then dry the sweetbreads and brains, cut them into small pieces and season with salt and pepper. Beat two of the eggs and dredge the pieces in egg and breadcrumbs, then fry them in hot olive oil, drain off the excess and put them on a plate.

Fry the diced potatoes and peppers in the oil remaining in the pan for about 15 minutes or until soft, then drain and reserve them.

Now beat the remaining six eggs in a bowl, add the fried ingredients and check the seasoning.

Clean the pan, pour in a little olive oil and heat until really hot. Add the contents of the bowl and cook first on one side and then on the other, exactly like a *tortilla española* (see pages 56-7). When finished the omelette should be browned on the outside and soft in the middle.

Perdices a la torera
Bullfighter's partridge

Serves 2.

2 partridge
2 oz (60 g) green bacon, chopped fine
2 oz (60 g) anchovies, cut up fine
2 large tomatoes, sliced
1 large green pepper, cut up
1 tablespoon chopped parsley
Salt and pepper
1 glass dry white wine
2 rashers ham

Stuff the partridge with the finely chopped bacon and anchovies, then put them in a stewpot, surrounded by the sliced tomatoes and cut-up pepper. Add the parsley and season with salt and pepper. Pour on the white wine and stew for 1 hour, adding a little more wine if necessary – but the amount of liquid should be small.

Fry the rashers of ham at the last moment, place the partridge on them and serve piping hot.

Liadillos sevillanos
Stuffed cabbage Seville style

12 leaves of white cabbage
Olive oil
2 oz (60 g) *tocino* or fresh belly of pork, cut up
2 oz (60 g) ham, chopped
10 black olives, stoned and chopped
3½ oz (100 g) minced veal, beef or pork, etc. (from a roast)
Nutmeg
Salt
2 eggs, beaten
Breadcrumbs

Wash the cabbage leaves and boil them in salted water for 10 minutes, taking care that they do not break. Drain them and leave them to cool on a clean cloth.

Put a little olive oil into a pan, fry together the belly of pork, ham and olives for about 15 minutes, then stir in the minced meat and season with nutmeg and salt.

Put a little of this mixture on each leaf and wrap it around, securing it either with a cocktail stick or with thread – which must be removed before serving. Dredge the filled leaves in beaten egg and breadcrumbs, fry in hot oil and remove any excess on kitchen paper before serving.

Ajoharina de Jaen
Spiced potatoes from Jaen

These spicy, orange-coloured potatoes are often eaten as a starter in Spain, but may also be served with roasts.

Olive oil
1 chilli, deseeded
2 lb (1 kg) potatoes, peeled and cut up
1 tablespoon sweet paprika powder
2 cloves garlic
1 heaped dessertspoon flour
Salt

Heat some olive oil in a pan and fry the chilli for about 5 minutes, then remove it and put it on a plate. Using the same oil, fry the potatoes and sprinkle on the sweet paprika. Now cover them with water and cook gently for 20 minutes.

Grind the garlic in a mortar, together with the fried chilli and the flour. Add a little of the stock from the potatoes so as to thin the paste, then add it to the potatoes in the pan. Stir well, season with salt and serve very hot.

Riñones al Jerez
Kidneys in sherry

2 lb (1 kg) calf's or pig's kidneys
2 tablespoons olive oil
1 small glass dry sherry
½ pint (3 dl) tomato sauce (see page 52)
Salt and pepper

Choose very tender kidneys, remove the skin and fat and cut them into slices with scissors. Heat the olive oil in a pan, sauté the kidneys for 5 minutes over a high flame, then put them in a colander to rid them of water. Now put the sautéed kidneys and sherry into a clean saucepan, add the tomato sauce, season with salt and pepper and cook very slowly until tender. The time varies according to whether they are calf's or pig's kidneys; 10 minutes are usually sufficient, but the best thing is to sample them. Serve with boiled white rice.

Polvorones sevillanos

These dry, powdery sweetmeats are often served with sherry.

13 oz (375 g) flour
6 oz (180 g) pork fat
2½ oz (75 g) caster sugar
1 small glass *aguardiente* (see page 147) or
  brandy
1 tablespoon ground cinnamon
Icing sugar

Pour the flour into a fireproof dish and heat in a hot oven until brown, stirring it at intervals and without allowing it to become too dark in colour. Remove and allow to cool.

Meanwhile beat the caster sugar with the pork fat until they are thoroughly mixed, add the *aguardiente* and cinnamon and then the flour, little by little, working it with a wooden spoon or palette knife. Now knead thoroughly with the fingers until the paste is smooth and leave it to rest for 20 minutes.

Roll out the dough on a pastry board or marble slab to a thickness of ⅓ inch (1 cm). Cut out circles with the top of a small glass, sprinkle them with a little flour, then place them in a greased baking tin and cook in a hot oven (425° F/220° C/ Mark 7) for about 10 minutes or until golden. Remove, powder with icing sugar and wrap in pieces of tissue paper, twisting the ends.

Levante

The Spanish Levante is of course not to be confused with the Levant of the eastern Mediterranean; it comprises the coastal strip stretching along the Mediterranean shore of Spain from the Cabo de Gato, just east of Almería, to the delta of the Ebro in the north. What gives the area geographical unity is the fertile, semi-tropical plain extending back from the sea, sometimes as much as forty kilometres, to the mountains ringing the high interior plateau.

It is a region of sweet-smelling orange and lemon groves, sugar cane, ricefields and palms; and not unnaturally its mild climate and rich soil attracted colonists from the Ancient World. The Phoenicians, Greeks and Carthaginians were all here in strength; and as Rose Macaulay has so evocatively written, 'This is a haunted shore: ghosts crowd each bay, each little town, each castled rock, whispering in the lap of the waves and in the low rumour of the sea wind in the palms.'

The sacking of Sagunto (the Saguntum of the Romans), just north of Valencia, by Hannibal in 219 BC precipitated the Second Punic War and the occupation of the Peninsula by the Romans. The area subsequently came under the sway of the Umayyad emirs and caliphs of Córdoba and after the collapse of the caliphate broke up into a number of independent Moorish principalities, of which the largest was Valencia. Valencia del Cid, as it is still sometimes called, enshrines the memory of the legendary hero, who, with his friend and enemy Alfonso VI of Castile, was one of the twin architects of the Christian Reconquest during the eleventh century.

After quarrelling with Alfonso, the Cid was banished from Castile and rode out from Burgos with a handful of followers to undertake the conquest of the Levante, culminating in the capture of Valencia. In the wake of a twenty-month siege, which reduced the beleaguered inhabitants to scouring the drains for olive stones and eating the flesh of mules and rats, the city fell to the Cid in June 1094 and remained his headquarters until his death in 1099, after which Alfonso ordered its evacuation in the face of a renewed Berber invasion from North Africa. When the region was finally reoccupied by the Christians it was not at the hand of the Castilians, but of another great soldier, James the Conqueror of Aragon-Catalonia, who re-took Valencia in 1238.

The influence of the Moriscos (Moors who were Christianized, at any rate in name) is still evident today, not least in the blue-tiled domes of the churches, rising above the white houses of the villages and towns, and in the low arched aqueducts and the cisterns for irrigating the fields. The manufacture of ceramics and tiles, of which the most typical are perhaps the *azulejos*, with their high glaze and designs in an intense blue on a white ground, was brought to a fine art by the Moriscos, and they are still made by the traditional methods. Valencia possesses the best ceramics museum in Spain, installed in the Baroque palace of the Marqués de dos Aguas; and one of its features is a traditional Valencian kitchen, with tiled walls and fireplace and a complete *batterie de cuisine*.

The city of Valencia, surrounded by its orange and lemon groves, is the queen of the Levante, and despite the devastation of the Napoleonic and Civil Wars, parts of the old wall with its gates and turrets, and narrow streets flanked by balconied houses still remain. It is the gastronomic centre of the Levante and the birthplace of *paella* (see pages 33 and 38), which is cooked to perfection in its numerous bars and restaurants, although it is now to Spain what roast beef is to England and is made and served all over the country in its manifold guises.

The other large cities of the Levante, Murcia and Alicante, lie south of Valencia, and both are places of wide modern avenues fringed with palm trees, though Murcia has preserved its many churches with blue-tiled cupolas and some of its tortuous streets and old houses. Alicante is reputedly one of the mildest places in Spain during the winter, and its serried cafés, which face the wide harbour across a marble-paved promenade lined with palms, are among the pleasantest in the country to relax with a glass of sherry or montilla and the accompanying *tapas*.

The word *tapa* originally meant a 'cover' and perhaps originated in the custom of covering the glasses to keep out flies. Today it is used for the multiplicity of small dishes served as apéritifs with the drink. Especially in southern Spain, the custom was to serve a few olives, a wedge of cold *tortilla* (Spanish omelette), or a few prawns or anchovies with the compliments of the house. *Tapas*, except for the simplest, are no longer free; and the more substantial, such as inkfish, crisp-fried in rings or stuffed and fried in their own ink;

stuffed peppers; fried fresh anchovies; mussels in marinade; shellfish like the delicious *percebes* (a form of edible barnacle); or Russian salad, are no longer cheap. Nevertheless, by choosing from the assortment of dishes, both hot and cold, lining the top of any bar, one can make a most appetizing lunch.

North of Valencia and back from the coast, the isolated Maestrazgo is a region apart from the rest of the Levante and this is reflected in its cooking. Until fairly recently it was difficult to bring fresh fish from the coast up the steep mountain tracks. The inhabitants cured a great deal of meat for consumption in the winter: *cecina* and *somarro*, dried salted beef and mutton, are well-known local specialities; and the cured ham is also excellent. In wet weather the stalls in the markets are piled with *robellones*, mushrooms of a flavour almost forgotten in these days of the mass-produced button variety; and there are some good local cheeses, such as that of Tronchón, mentioned in *Don Quixote*.

The Levante in general and Valencia in particular are famous for a great variety of rice dishes, often made with the abundant fish from the Mediterranean, but also with vegetables or meat. The original *paella* contained only eels, snails and shelled green beans in addition to rice. These eels came from the large salt-water lagoon of the Albufera, south-east of Valencia – from which Marshal Suchet took his title of Duke of Albufera after capturing the city for Napoleon in 1812 – and the rice was provided from the swampy fields on its borders. It was traditionally cooked in a large *cazuela*, a round dish made of brown earthenware, glazed on the inside but not on the bottom, which was set on a wood fire.

Cazuelas in all sizes and depths, from the small, shallow dishes used for making *huevos a la flamenca* (see page 25) to pots capacious enough to make a stew for a family of twelve, may be bought in shops and markets all over Spain, and, inexpensive as they are, it is well worth bringing home a set if you are travelling by car and weight is no problem. Apart from their decorative appearance and heat-retaining properties, they are excellent cooking vessels, since they preserve the flavour of the ingredients better than pots and pans made of metal and may be heated directly over a gas ring if you are careful. To prevent a new *cazuela* from cracking over the fire, rub the unglazed base with two or three cloves of garlic, and when the juice has been absorbed, pour in some water and bring it slowly to the boil. Throw away the water, and the *cazuela* is ready for use.

It is easier to cook a *paella* in the two-handled metal *paellera* now generally used for the purpose. It, too, is most decorative and may be brought to the table, unlike an ordinary frying pan.

The best modern alternative to *cazuelas* is the range of French or

Swedish pans and stewpots made of heavy cast metal and stove-enamelled on the inside, which may safely be heated on a gas ring.

The ingredients that may be put to use in a *paella* are legion, and Dionisio Pérez writes in his *Guía del buen comer español* that 'failing the classical ingredients, each locality in the Kingdom of Valencia and each village in the neighbouring provinces has put into the *paella* every form of meat, fish, shellfish and fresh vegetable; and the marvellous rice goes well with all of them'.

The secret, of course, *is* in the cooking of the saffron-flavoured rice, whose grains, though tender, must remain individual when the dish is brought to the table. For this purpose it is essential to start with the round-grained Spanish or Italian rice – the fluffy white Indian or American varieties make excellent rice pudding or curry, but not *paella*. The amount of water used in cooking it is all-important. The traditional method was to put the rice with a little water into the *paellera* and to heat it over a high flame, meanwhile adding more water gradually and stirring with a wooden spoon. To begin with, the spoon will stand upright in the mounded rice; when it begins to slump under its own weight, it is a sign that sufficient water has been added. Heating should be steady, otherwise the grains will tend to disintegrate; and once all the water has either evaporated or been absorbed, the *paellera* must be removed from the fire and left to stand for some minutes, so that the moisture penetrates to the heart of the grains and softens them all through. An easier method of gauging the correct amount of water, by measuring two cupfuls to each cupful of dry rice, is described in the recipe on page 39.

Cut-up pieces of chicken, small sausages and small pieces of cooked meat are all useful ingredients for *paella*; but perhaps the most satisfactory version is *paella marinera* made entirely with shellfish, apart, of course, from the usual garnish of olives and strips of red pepper. This is also cooked well along the Basque coast, with its superb fish from the Atlantic, in restaurants like that of the Parador del Emperador at Fuenterrabía near the French border. But be on your guard: the most expensive restaurants with the best shellfish can make deplorable *paellas*, and unless the rice is properly prepared, the dish is a disaster.

A great variety of Mediterranean fish is caught off the coast of the Levante: to see it in all its variety, from heaped piles of prawns, red mullet, sardines and *langoustines* to squid, octopus or exotics such as *rascasio* –the ugly *rascasse* so essential to *bouillabaisse* –tour the stalls of a big fish market in one of the larger ports such as Castellón de la Plana. One variety of shellfish is so unusual to deserve special mention. You will occasionally see on a menu *sopa de dátiles* (page 118); this does not, as you might think, mean 'date soup', but refers to a particularly delicious chowder made from a small and very rare dark brown mussel (*dáil de mar*) fished off the coast near Péñiscola and Benicarló.

The *huertas* or 'gardens' of Valencia are proverbial for their fertility, and justifiably so, since there are two crops of vegetables and oranges a year. One of the region's most important industries is the export of spring vegetables – as becomes only too painfully obvious when one is caught along the main coast road in a convoy of trucks carrying beans, peas or greens to the markets of France. Unlike those from Seville, the oranges are of the sweet variety and range in size from large navels to tangerines or the seedless *celestinas* exported in large quantity to Japan for making crystallized fruit. In springtime one can drive for mile upon mile through the dark green citrus groves along roads heavy with the scent of blossom, but oranges and lemons are far from being the only fruit: figs, both green and black, are so prolific that they are sometimes fed to the pigs; and among the exotics are dates, pomegranates, passionfruit and loquats. The coastal area between Valencia and Alicante is famous for its muscatelle grapes; and until the Civil War there was a thriving British community in the small port of Denia, occupied in the export of raisins. Almonds are another favourite crop, since they form the basis for so many of the sweetmeats made in the Levante, as in Andalusia, since the time of the Moors.

The most famous of such is *turrón*, a nougat traditionally packed in small wooden boxes, like those used for liqueur chocolates, and eaten at Christmas time. It is now hermetically sealed in tins and exported all over the world. There is a story that it takes its name from a Don Joseph Terrón of Alicante, who won the prize in a competition organized by King Ferdinand VII, after he returned from his exile in France during the Peninsular War, with a confection of honey and chopped almonds. However, it seems entirely likely that Sr Terrón was elaborating on an earlier form of Moorish sweetmeat, since there is an old rhyme about *giraboix*, as it is called in Jijona, where most of it is made:

Si la reina saber
lo que es giraboix,
a Xixona vendría
a llepar el boix
[If the queen knew
Turrón and its taste,
She'd go to Jijona
To lick it in haste].

Jijona, a small mountain town north of Alicante, is completely given over to the confection of *turrón*; there are some forty small manufactories scattered along its hilly streets and the whole place is redolent with the comforting aroma of toasted almonds and honey. There are two main types. The *turrón de Alicante*, made from almonds, toasted and coarsely chopped, sugar, honey and whites of egg, is brittle and must be broken into lumps. The *turrón de Jijona*, equally delicious and made from ground almonds, ground pine kernels, sugar, coriander and egg yolks, is a soft tablet and kinder on the teeth. Neither may be made with any success at home, but the somewhat similar *Guirlache*, also popular in Aragon, presents no difficulty, and a recipe follows (page 44).

The Levante produces an enormous amount of wine, both red and white, and in the 1851 edition of his now classical *History and Description of Modern Wines* Cyrus Redding wrote glowingly of their promising future. He was perhaps unduly influenced by the astonishing fertility of the soil and the long summers with their unbroken sunshine. In sober fact the vine is a plant which flourishes in a more barren habitat, such as the chalky *albarizas* of Jerez, and excessive heat results in very large amounts of sugar in the fruit and wines overstrong in alcohol. The alluvial soils of the Levante plain are ideal for growing the dessert Moscatel, but it is in the more temperate north that Spain makes its best table wines.

All the wines from the coastal areas of Murcia, Alicante, Valencia and Castellón de la Plana tend to be heavy, 'earthy' in taste and high in alcohol. Perhaps the champion heavyweights are the red wines from Jumilla and Yecla, inky black in colour and containing some 18° (18 per cent by volume) of alcohol – at which point the yeasts which break down the sugar are paralysed. This is not to say that they lack character or are not most acceptable with highly-flavoured food or on a picnic with a *bocadillo*, a crusty roll containing *jamón serrano*, the spiced *chorizo* sausage or a slice of cold *tortilla*. It is incidentally the universal custom in Spain to drink red wine with *paella*, since white does not stand up to its full flavour.

Utiel and Requena, off the main road from Valencia to Madrid and in the cooler mountain region on the edge of the central plateau, make lighter red wines containing some 11° to 12° of alcohol. They were the favourite of the Valencian-born Vicente Blasco Ibáñez, who indeed wrote a novel called *La Bodega* but is more famous as the author of *The Four Horsemen of the Apocalypse*.

Because of its stout body and high alcohol content, wine from the Levante has always been in demand for blending with less robust growths from the north, and the trade was at its peak during the later years of the nineteenth century. A great deal of wine is still shipped from the great bodegas of Alicante and Valencia, and much of it finds its way to Tarragona, where it is used for making up Spanish 'Chablis' or 'Burgundy'.

The strangest case was that of the wine from Benicarló in the north of the Levante near the Catalonian border, in the words of Richard Ford, 'the well-known black strap, which is exported largely to Bordeaux to enrich clarets for our vitiated taste'. The custom arose because, as a result of the Methuen Treaty of 1703, which gave preference to wines from Portugal, English palates had become used to strong, full-bodied red wine. Even a London wine merchant as reputable as the conscientious Nathaniel Johnson would 'fret' a tun of his Bordeaux with a few gallons of Spanish wine. 'I loves a good strong generous wine,' said the hero of *Jorrocks' Jaunts and Jollities*, and half-measures in no way met his taste: 'It's not werry good, I think, if it were not claret I would sooner drink port.'

A refreshing alternative to alcoholic drinks during the long hot summer is *horchata valenciana*. This is made by macerating *chufas*, small wrinkled earth-nuts, somewhat like truffles in appearance, and is served as an ice-cold milky liquid in many bars, both in the Levante and further afield.

Recipes

Ensalada levantina
Salad from the Levante

1 clove garlic
2 hard-boiled eggs
1 slice bread
½ teacup olive oil
1 tablespoon vinegar (or to taste)
Salt
1 lettuce, washed and dried

Crush the garlic into a bowl and add the chopped egg yolks. Soak the bread in the mixed oil and vinegar for 5 minutes and make a paste of it. Stir this little by little into the bowl as if making mayonnaise. Season and pour over the lettuce, finally sprinkling it with the chopped whites of egg.

Robellones al estilo del Maestrazgo
Mushrooms Maestrazgo style

Serves 2.

2 oz (60 g) pork fat
½ lb (225 g) mushrooms, quartered
4 cloves garlic, crushed
2 tablespoons chopped parsley
Salt
Black pepper, freshly ground

Heat the pork fat in a pan and cook the mushrooms over a low fire, stirring them gently. Add the crushed garlic and the parsley, continue stirring slowly, season with salt and black pepper and serve at once.

Faves al Tombet
Broad beans Alicante style

1 lettuce, washed and shredded
2 lb (1 kg) fresh broad beans, shelled
Olive oil
2 cloves garlic
1 slice bread
1 teaspoon vinegar
½ teaspoon sweet paprika powder
Salt and pepper

Mix the shredded lettuce and broad beans. Heat a little olive oil in a stewpan and fry the cloves of garlic until golden. Transfer them to a mortar and grind into a paste with the bread, adding a teaspoon of vinegar and another of water. Using the same pan and oil, cook the lettuce and beans, adding sufficient water to simmer the vegetables for about 20 minutes, or until the beans are tender. Add the mixture of garlic and bread and the teaspoon of sweet paprika, stir well and season with salt and white pepper. This dish should be juicy, but not thin like a soup.

Paella valenciana

The beauty of *paella* is that, provided the rice is properly cooked and seasoned, it may be made with a wide variety of other ingredients. Take your choice of those listed below – the bigger the variety, the more exciting the final result – or, if you prefer, make it simply with chicken. There are people who take a dislike to inkfish simply on sight, but it is an important ingredient in a *paella marinera* (one made entirely with fish), since it gives the rice a very good flavour; when cut up and mixed with the rice its presence is hardly noticeable.

2 spring chickens or 1 chicken of 2–3 lb (1–1½ kg)
Flour
Olive oil
1 lb (½ kg) small inkfish (squid)
2 lb (1 kg) mussels
Garlic
Rice (1 cup per person)
Pinch of saffron
Salt
Shellfish, e.g. prawns, crayfish, lobster, crab
1 large can red peppers, cut into strips
Green or black olives

Cut up the chicken, dredge with flour, brown lightly in hot olive oil and reserve.

Clean the inkfish (see page 24), then cut them into small pieces, fry in olive oil for about 10 minutes until tender and reserve.

Soak the mussels in water, scrape the shells with a knife and scrub them until thoroughly clean, discarding any that are open. Now put them in a large saucepan with a little water, cover and bring to the boil to open them. Any that do *not* open at this stage are not fit for eating. Take them out with a draining spoon and allow them to cool on a plate, then remove them from their shells, keeping the best half-shells for decoration. Strain the stock from the mussels through muslin to remove grit and keep for further use.

Heat two tablespoons of olive oil in a *paellera* (see page 32) or large frying pan and fry two or three slices from a clove of garlic until they begin to brown. Discard them and add one cupful per person of round Spanish or Italian rice – if you use the fluffy white, long-grained variety, you will end up with something more like rice pudding than *paella* – and fry it gently until it begins to yellow.

Meanwhile, grind together a clove of garlic and a pinch of saffron in a mortar, scatter the mixture over the frying rice and season with salt.

The liquid for boiling the rice is made up of the strained mussel stock with as much additional water as is required. The total amount should be two cupfuls per person, i.e. exactly twice the volume of the dry rice. Add this now, stirring for 5 minutes as it begins to boil and bubble through the rice.

Stir in the inkfish and place the pieces of chicken around the edges of the pan.

Allow the rice, inkfish and chicken to cook together for 15 minutes, then decorate the top with the other ingredients: first the shellfish, then the strips of red pepper and finally the olives.

Last of all, replace the mussels in the best of their half-shells and garnish the dish with them.

Now remove the pan from the fire and cover it with a clean tea cloth for about 10 minutes before serving. A well-made *paella* is a most colourful and decorative sight, and one of the advantages of using a *paellera* is that it may be brought to the table.

Arroz a la marinera al estilo de Levante
Rice with fish Levante style

4 tablespoons olive oil
14 oz (400 g) white fish, cleaned and cut up
14 oz (400 g) rice
Pinch of sweet paprika powder
2 cloves garlic
1 small packet saffron
Salt
3 canned red peppers, cut into strips

Heat the olive oil in a *paellera* or large frying pan and fry the fish for about 5 minutes until golden, then stir in the rice with a wooden spoon and add the paprika powder and a measured amount of water equal to twice the dry volume of the rice. Grind the garlic and filaments of saffron in a mortar, add to the pan and season with salt. Cook slowly for a further 20 minutes and decorate with the strips of red pepper. Cover with a clean tea cloth and leave for 10 minutes before serving.

ARROZ ABANDA

This rice dish is almost as famous in Valencia as *paella*.

Olive oil
1 onion, chopped
4 tomatoes, chopped
Bouquet garni of thyme, bay leaf and parsley
Salt and pepper
½ lb (225 g) Dublin Bay prawns
½ lb (225 g) prawns
1 small packet saffron
1 lb (½ kg) halibut or other firm white fish
1 lb (½ kg) angler fish
1 dozen clams
2 cloves garlic
1 cup per person round-grained Spanish or Italian rice
Salt
Mayonnaise to serve on the side

If it has not been done already, boil the prawns and reserve the stock.

Heat a little olive oil in a pan, fry half of the chopped onion until it changes colour and add two of the chopped tomatoes. Cook gently for 10 minutes, then add 2½ pints (1½ litres) of water and the *bouquet garni*. Season with salt and pepper, add the heads and shells of the prawns and continue gentle cooking for ½ hour. Strain through a sieve and reserve the stock.

Clean and cut up the white fish and the angler fish and put the pieces together with the clams into a saucepan with the stock. Grind and add the packet of saffron and simmer for 10 minutes, then remove the fish with a draining spoon and arrange it on a serving dish with the prawns, again reserving the stock for further use.

Now take a *paellera* or large pan, heat a little oil in it, add the remainder of the chopped onions and tomatoes and the chopped garlic, and fry the rice until golden. Measure out the fish stock in the proportion of two parts by volume to one of the dry rice, adding a little water if there is not enough stock. Pour the liquid over the rice and boil gently for 5 minutes. Now place the pan in a hot oven (400° F/200° C/Mark 6), bake for 15 minutes, then turn off the heat and leave the pan in the oven for another 10 minutes before serving.

The rice and the fish are served separately with mayonnaise on the side.

Sardinas al estilo de Cartagena
Sardines in tomato sauce

This unusual way of cooking fresh sardines originated in the seaport of Cartagena. The fish are layered with a piquant vegetable relish and fried in a tomato sauce.

Sauce

Olive oil
1 onion, chopped
14 oz (400 g) can of tomatoes
Salt

Heat a little olive oil in a pan and fry the finely chopped onion until golden. Drain off any excess oil, add the tomatoes and continue slow frying for 15 minutes. Season with salt, rub through a sieve or put into the blender and reserve.

Vegetable relish

3 red peppers, cut up fine
1 onion, finely chopped
2 cloves garlic, crushed
1 tablespoon parsley, chopped
Salt and pepper
1 small packet saffron, ground

Thoroughly mix together all the vegetables and reserve.

Fish

20 fresh sardines
1 tablespoon refined olive oil

Clean and wash the sardines, slitting them along one edge, opening them flat and removing the backbones. Pour the tomato sauce into a large earthenware *cazuela* or metal fish pan, place the first layer of opened sardines on top and cover them with vegetable relish. Continue with alternate layers of fish and relish and finally sprinkle a tablespoon of olive oil over the top. Cook slowly on top of the stove for ¼ hour, shaking from time to time.

Atun valenciano
Tuna fish Valencian style

Any firm white fish may be used for this recipe.

8 slices fresh tuna (2 per person)
Salt and pepper
Flour
Olive oil
2 cloves garlic
1 tablespoon chopped parsley
2 small packets saffron
1 tablespoon dry white wine

Sprinkle the slices of fish with a little salt and pepper, dredge them in flour and fry them a few at a time in hot olive oil for 5 minutes each side until golden. Transfer the pieces as they are cooked to a saucepan. Meanwhile grind the garlic, parsley and saffron in a mortar, stir in the white wine and pour the mixture over the fish. Simmer for 10 minutes, check the seasoning and serve.

Empanadillas valencianas
Valencian fish pasties

Savoury and golden brown, these somewhat resemble Cornish pasties in appearance.

Pastry
1 teacup olive oil
1 tablespoon anisette or Pernod
Salt
Flour

Pour the olive oil and anisette into a large bowl and mix well with a wooden spoon. Add a teacup of tepid water and a little salt and then, beating all the time, add enough flour to make a paste which may be kneaded with the fingers as if making bread. Cover the bowl and leave to rest for ½ hour.

Filling
½ lb (225 g) tomatoes, blanched and peeled
8 oz (225 g) smoked fillet of haddock or an 8 oz (225 g) can of tuna
Salt and pepper

If smoked haddock is used, it must first be poached in milk for 10 minutes, skinned and boned.

Put the peeled tomatoes in a frying pan and cook gently for 10 to 15 minutes to make a thick purée. Season with salt and pepper, stir in the flaked fish and allow to cool.

Roll out the dough into a thin sheet on a floured pastry board or marble slab and measure out dollops of the filling with a tablespoon. Cut around them with a pastry cutter and fold over the dough in the shape of pasties, sealing the edges with a fork. Roll out the remains of the dough again when necessary and continue until all the dough and filling have been used.

Fry in hot olive oil or bake in a hot oven until the pasties are golden brown. Serve either hot or cold with a green salad. If made smaller, they may also be served as a starter or at a cocktail party.

Conejo a la valenciana
Rabbit Valencian style

Olive oil
2 lb (1 kg) rabbit, cut into small pieces
Flour
1 green pepper, deseeded and chopped
3 cloves garlic, chopped
Sprig of parsley
Salt and pepper
1 pint (6 dl) meat stock (or water)

Heat a little olive oil in a pan, dredge the pieces of rabbit in flour, fry them until browned and transfer them with a draining spoon to a stewpot.

Using the same pan and oil, fry the chopped pepper, garlic and parsley, seasoning the mixture with salt and pepper. Add the stock or water, stir well and pour over the pieces of rabbit in the stewpot. Bring to the boil and simmer slowly for about 1 hour or, if necessary, rather longer.

Bizcocho de naranja
Orange cake

4 oz (125 g) butter
3½ oz (100 g) icing sugar
3 eggs
6 oz (180 g) candied orange peel
Peel of 1 orange, grated
1 liqueur glass rum
3½ oz (100 g) flour
3 oz (80 g) potato flour

Leave out the butter to soften, then beat it in a bowl with the sugar until smooth. Beat in the eggs one by one and add the candied and grated orange peel and rum. Mix and sieve the two types of flour and incorporate into the other ingredients to make a smooth paste. Now put it into a greased baking tin and cook for ½ to ¾ hour in a medium oven (350° F/180° C/Mark 4). Allow the cake to cool before turning it out on to a serving dish.

Naranjas acarameladas
Caramelized oranges

Oranges
4 oz (110 g) caster sugar
2 tablespoons water

Peel the oranges, cut them into quarters and leave them for 2 hours, so that they dry a little. Now make the caramel by heating the sugar in water until light brown. Stir in the quartered oranges, then remove the segments with a draining spoon and leave them on a plate to cool. Serve in the shape of a pyramid.

Turron de Guirlache
Nougat Guirlache

1 lb (450 g) caster sugar
3½ oz (100 g) mixed pork fat and olive oil
2 oz (50 g) toasted almonds, ground

Heat the sugar and mixed fat and oil in a small heavy saucepan, and when the sugar begins to melt add the ground almonds, stirring well with a wooden spoon. Cook gently for two or three minutes, then pour the mixture into a small greased cake tin (it is easier to remove the *turrón*, when set, from a tin with a detachable base). Allow it to

cool and cut it into fingers while still soft.
Serve as a dessert or with coffee.

TURRON DE CASTAÑAS
CHESTNUT NOUGAT

Another version of *turrón*, which may successfully be made at home.

1 lb (½ kg) chestnuts, peeled
Milk
3 oz (85 g) unsalted butter
3 oz (85 g) cooking chocolate, grated
3 oz (85 g) caster sugar, vanilla flavoured

Bring the chestnuts to the boil in water, then take them from the pan and remove the inner skins. Now cover them with milk and simmer for about 20 minutes until tender. While the chestnuts are still warm, rub them through a sieve and mix them thoroughly in a large bowl with all the other ingredients so as to make a smooth paste. Line an ice tray with cooking foil, smooth in the mixture and leave in the refrigerator until the following day. Serve with cream.

VALENCIANOS.

New Castile

Between them, the two Castiles occupy the great central plateau of Spain. Old Castile, which was so called because it was the first part of the area to be reconquered from the Moors, stretches northwards from Madrid. South of the capital the landscape becomes increasingly arid, and the southern part of New Castile, bordering the Sierra Morena and Andalusia, is known as La Mancha. Its desolate and rolling plains, relieved by the occasional white-washed village or clustered windmills, are Don Quixote country; and Cervantes mirrors the tough fibre and frugal character of its inhabitants when he writes of his hero:

> In a place of La Mancha, whose name I do not remember, there lived not long ago one of those gentlemen who boasts a wooden lance and old buckler, a scraggy horse and a greyhound for coursing. An *olla* [stew] containing more cow's meat than mutton, scratch fare most nights, grief and bickering on Saturdays, lentils on Fridays and perhaps a pigeon on Sundays consumed three quarters of his substance . . .

The historical capital of New Castile is Toledo, for long occupied by the Moors, and whose recapture in 1085 was the single greatest achievement of Alfonso VI. The city was of transcendent importance in transmitting the learning of the ancient Greeks and the Arabs to Western Europe, from the time that a canon of its cathedral, Domingo Gonzalvo, founded a school of translators towards the end of the eleventh century until its final flowering under Alfonso X ('the Wise'), who ruled Castile from 1252-84. Toledo was later the adopted home of El Greco; and his house, now a museum containing some of his paintings, still stands. Seeing the city from a distance against a thundery sky, with the lightning striking down towards the jagged outline of its towers and spires, one might even today be looking at one of his canvases.

Toledo has long since yielded pride of place to Madrid, but the present capital of Spain was a small place of little importance when it was recaptured by Alfonso VI in 1083. Thereafter it was the occasional scene for meetings of the Cortes (parliament); it was not until 1561 that Philip II, whose austere character matched the bleak expanses of his native Castile, made it capital of Spain. Even then, his son and successor, Philip III, abandoned it for Valladolid in 1601; but the Court returned in 1607, since when it has grown to be the largest city in Spain, attracting new inhabitants like a magnet. The magnificent Prado Museum was finished only after the end of the Peninsular War, during which Joseph Bonaparte demolished much of old Madrid; and its principal thoroughfare, the Avenida José Antonio or Gran Via, with the monumental Edwardian buildings that flank it, was constructed during the early years of the present century. Since then, new construction has proceeded apace, notably around the fashionable Paseo Castellana to the north and in the industrial outskirts. The larger part of the city is therefore comparatively modern.

Madrid has for long typified two styles of cooking: that of the aristocracy and upper classes; and the native, which is in effect that of New Castile. This is reflected in its restaurants, which have more recently been swelled by a third category catering to the tastes of newcomers from the other regions of Spain.

There is no dearth of restaurants serving the most sophisticated food: one need mention only such well-established favourites as The Jockey; Horcher; Mayte Commodore; the Ritz, one of the most perfect hotels in Europe; Bajamar, whose unsurpassed seafood is flown in daily from the north coast; or Valentín, more specifically Spanish in style and the rendezvous now, as in the past, of bullfighters, actors and writers.

Without going further afield you may sample well-cooked Galician dishes at O'Paxo; Valencian, at La Barraca or The Valencia; Basque, at Zarauz or Jai-Alai; or Andalusian, at La Chuleta – to mention only a few.

The regional food of New Castile is to be found in smaller and often quite humble restaurants, fittingly enough located in old Madrid in the area of the Puerta del Sol and the magnificent Plaza Mayor, with its Baroque arcades. Some of these places, such as Botín or the Mesón de San Javier, famous for its roast lamb, are household words. Another old-established Madrid restaurant, Lhardy, was mentioned with approval even by the exigent Alexandre Dumas:

So, Madame, our luncheon arrangements are settled. As for

> dinner, M. Monnier recommends us to try a restaurant owned by an Italian, Lardi by name, where we should be able to obtain a reasonably good meal. In Italy, where one has poor meals, the good inn-keepers are French; in Spain, where one finds no meals at all, the best inn-keepers are Italian . . .

Agustín de Lhardy, a descendant of the Italian founder, was ironically enough to become a protagonist in the struggle to re-establish the good name of the Spanish cuisine.

Without necessarily visiting one of these well-known places, a most enjoyable way of sampling the authentic cooking of New Castile is to make for the Calle Ventura de la Vega or the parallel Echegaray, narrow, old-fashioned streets off the main artery of Alcalá and within easy walking distance of the Prado. Here the tiled bodegas – which serve first-rate Valdepeñas from the barrel – and unpretentious eating places stand cheek by jowl, and you may take your pick.

Two phrases recur on their menus. *A la manchega* means simply that the recipe originated in La Mancha; *a la madrileña* was first used during the nineteenth century and was originally descriptive of dishes prepared quickly and simply to satisfy the impatience of the customers frequenting the numerous restaurants which sprang up at that time. People in big cities are notoriously in a hurry; and the tradition of quick service survives in the crowded and popular *cafeterías*, whose staples are substantial toasted sandwiches and *platos combinados*, akin to a mixed grill, in which a combination of fried meats, sausage, egg and chips; of cheese or egg salads; or of fish with various accompaniments, constitutes a complete meal.

Of the dishes typical of New Castile, mention must first be made of *sopa de ajo madrileña*, a soup made from garlic, bread and eggs, spiced with a little paprika, though it is not everyone who likes a soup tasting so strongly of garlic. The famous *cocido madrileño* is a dish, like *pot au feu*, in which vegetables and meat are stewed together and then eaten separately. First to be served is the broth; then the vegetables, which always include *garbanzos* (chick-peas) and generally potato and cabbage; and finally the assorted meat, chicken and spiced sausage. According to the variety of ingredients it is a dish which may be simple or complicated, like the *olla en grande*, of which Don Quixote remarked that it was eaten only by canons and presidents of colleges.

Akin to the *cocido* is the much simpler *potaje madrileño*, in its basic form a nourishing soup made with chick-peas and wild spinach, sometimes with the addition of *bacalao* (dried cod), and eaten during Lent. The basic recipe may be modified by the use of other dried vegetables, such as lentils or butter beans, and with the addition of the highly spiced *chorizo* this is a most acceptable and warming winter dish.

If these three essentially peasant dishes are typical of New Castile and the Madrid of earlier days, there now exists a whole gamut of less solid fare, of which the recipes that follow are representative.

Alexandre Dumas' first experience of the Spanish table was a breakfast-time cup of chocolate. He was not disappointed – though he complained bitterly that it was served in thimbles rather than cups. It was in the *chocolaterías* of Madrid, formerly open all night for the benefit of travellers and the homeless, that the *churro* (recipe on page 63) made its first appearance. These golden-brown fingers, made of a dough cooked in smoking olive oil, are now popular all over Spain for breakfast or a *merienda* (afternoon snack). They are made fresh each morning in *churrerías*, which later in the day produce the potato crisps, large, crisp, thick and of a flavour lost in the packaged variety, served in the bars and *cervecerías*. Not so long ago there was a *churrera* (*churro* seller) on every street corner of Madrid in the early morning, when the servants emerged to buy their wares for the household. Spain, like other countries, is now turning to convenience foods, such as the packaged '*Bimbo*' toast; but even the luxury hotels will still produce *churros* for breakfast, if you insist. A Manchegan and Andalusian variant of the *churro* is the *buñuelo*, for which yeast is mixed with dough; it is consequently lighter and emerges as a hollow tube.

The environs of Madrid and the outlying regions of New Castile all have their own gastronomic specialities. The roast lamb and sucking pig of Segovia are described in the chapter on Old Castile. Aranjuez on the River Manzanares, the site of a royal palace and gardens reminiscent of Versailles and the scene of dramatic events when Carlos IV and his debauched favourite, Godoy, were overturned on the eve of the Peninsular War, is famous for its strawberries and luscious asparagus. The melons, which appear in piles in the Madrid streets around September, hail from the village of Villaconejos. Along the dusty byroads of La Mancha you will see signs at every turn labelled '*coto privado*' ('hunting reserved'); the Sunday silence of the rolling sierra is punctuated by the crack of guns; and towards evening the little groups of hunters return with their pouches full of rabbit, partridge and quail.

La Mancha also produces the best-known Spanish cheese, Manchego. It is a hard cheese made from ewe's milk in large rounds and is sold all over the country. Without quite the bite of Cheddar, it nevertheless gains an intensity of flavour when matured in large jars of olive oil.

Toledo is as famous for its Moorish sweetmeats as for its tempered sword blades and is especially noteworthy for marzipan (see page 64), which was originally made at Christmas and fashioned into small figures. Marzipan is yet another recipe for which credit has been claimed by the French. The generally informative and reliable *Larousse Gastronomique* reproduces a circular issued in 1844 by a Paris confectionery, in which it was rumoured that the novelist Honoré de Balzac had an interest, advertising marzipan from Issoudon, and lends its weight to the proposition that the sweet was first devised by nuns in the Province of Berry. The fact that the name is derived from the Arabic *mawthapan* would seem to discredit this theory; and there is a well-founded tradition that it was first made some eight centuries earlier during the siege of Toledo by Alfonso VI, when the Moors were left with few provisions except bread, almonds and sugar. Egg white was a later addition.

Between them, the provinces of New Castile are the largest producers of wine in bulk in the whole of Spain. Apart from wheat, grapes are the region's biggest crop; the vineyards extend unbroken to the horizon; and dozens of townships, such as Ciudad Real, Méntrida, Ocana, Tomelloso and Alcázar de San Juan are largely given over to making wine or to distilling the surplus for brandy and liqueurs. Spanish brandy is not made like French by the distillation of wine made from grapes grown specially for the purpose, but is elaborated, mostly by the big sherry houses in Jerez de la Frontera, from *holandas* or grape spirit, much of which originates in New Castile. The little town of Chinchón, near Madrid, makes a first-rate anisette (the best-known mark is 'Anís del Mono') – and incidentally gave its name to quinine, since it was an eighteenth-century Marquesa de Chinchón, married to a Governor of Peru, who discovered the medicinal properties of cinchona bark, from which quinine is extracted.

The wine centre of New Castile is Valdepeñas (originally *Val de Peñas*, the 'valley of stones'), lying on the southern fringe of La Mancha, close to the border with Andalusia. The lively and brisk red Valdepeñas and the *aloques*, made from a mixture of black and white grapes, are wines with a history going back to Roman times and are still made in large earthenware vessels similar in shape to the Roman amphorae. Valdepeñas was the mother's milk of Sancho Panza, of which he declared: '*Bebo cuando tengo gana, cuando no la tengo y cuando me lo dan, por no parecer melindroso o mal criado*' (I drink it when I have the taste and also when they give it to me and I do not, so as not to seem offhand or bad-mannered).

The Emperor Charles V was such an addict that he had the wine transported across Europe on mule-back during his campaigns in the Low Countries. Alexandre Dumas went to a great deal of trouble to obtain the genuine article, which was not always easy. His contemporary, Richard Ford, remarks that:

> . . . it is apt, when conveyed in skins, to be tapped and watered by the muleteers, besides imbibing the disagreeable smack of pitched pigskin. The only way to secure a pure, unadulterated, legitimate article, is to send up *double* quarter sherry casks; the wine is put in one, and that again is protected by an outer cask, which acts as a preventive guard, against gimlets, straws, and other ingenious contrivances for extracting the vinous contents, and for introducing an aqueous substitute.

Valdepeñas was much in demand for making good supplies during the phylloxera epidemic of the late nineteenth century in France and is today the stable carafe wine of Madrid. And very good it is, fresh, fruity and surprisingly light considering its high degree of alcohol.

Recipes

SALSA ESPAÑOLA

This is the staple sauce of Spanish cookery, used in a great variety of different dishes, of which Richard Ford wrote that 'to change this sauce would be little short of heresy', adding that 'its *negro de hueso* colour is the livery of tawny Spain, where all is brown from the *Sierra Morena* to duskier man. Of such hue is his cloak, his terra cotta house, his wife, his ox, his ass, and everything that is his.'

3½ fl. oz (1 dl) olive oil
1 onion, chopped
2 carrots, chopped
7 oz (200 g) beef bones, chopped up
1¼ oz (35 g) flour
1 tomato, cut up
3½ fl. oz (1 dl) white wine
Salt

Heat a little olive oil in a pan and brown the onion, together with the carrots and beef bones, then stir in the flour with a wooden spoon. Add the chopped tomato and then transfer to a saucepan containing 1¼ pints (¾ litre) of water, the white wine and a little salt. Simmer gently until reduced to the required volume and strain through a kitchen sieve, retaining only the liquid.

The sauce may be kept in the refrigerator in a well-stoppered container and used in small amounts as required.

Adobo a la madrileña
Marinade for pork

This marinade is used for flavouring the meat, especially chops and loin.

1 clove garlic, crushed
Pinch of salt
½ teaspoon paprika powder
½ teacup olive oil
½ teacup dry white wine
2 tablespoons vinegar
Bay leaf, chopped
Pinch of origanum
Pinch of black pepper

Make a paste by grinding and blending all the ingredients in a mortar. Transfer to a dish, cover and keep in the refrigerator for at least four to five hours. It should be used sparingly.

Ensalada manchega
A salad from La Mancha

This is served as a starter.

Salad
1 oz (30 g) *bacalao* (dried and salted cod)
7½ oz (215 g) can of tuna, drained and flaked
2 hard-boiled eggs
2 large tomatoes, blanched, peeled and chopped
1 onion, thinly sliced
12 olives, green or black, stoned

Dressing
4 dessertspoons (50 ml) refined olive oil
2 dessertspoons (25 ml) vinegar or lemon juice
½ teaspoon French mustard
1 clove garlic, squeezed
Salt and pepper

The *bacalao* must be soaked overnight. The following morning, rinse it, remove skin and bones, then flake it.

First put the tuna and chopped hard-boiled eggs into a salad bowl, then add the tomatoes (which will be a bit runny after chopping), the sliced onion, olives and *bacalao*. Mix the dressing, pour it on top and toss well before serving.

Sopa de ajo con huevos
Garlic soup with eggs

This is the recipe transcribed by Alexandre Dumas, although he omitted the paprika, with which it is usually seasoned in Spain.

A little olive oil
4 cloves garlic, finely chopped
1 tablespoon sweet paprika powder
7 oz (200 g) stale bread, sliced thin
1¾ pints (1 litre) broth or water
Salt
3 eggs, beaten

Heat the olive oil in a large saucepan and fry the garlic very briefly, taking care that it does not blacken. As soon as it changes colour add the paprika, the bread and the water or broth. Simmer for about 5 minutes, season with salt. Stir in the beaten egg and it is ready to serve.

In its native Castile the soup is often made in a large earthenware *cazuela* (see page 32). After the addition of the beaten egg this is put under the grill or in the oven for 10 minutes, when the soup acquires a golden colour as the egg cooks and coagulates.

Sopa toledana
Toledan soup

1 tablespoon olive oil
1 lb (½ kg) spinach, cooked and chopped
Salt
2 beaten eggs
1 tablespoon grated cheese
1¼ pints (¾ litre) broth
4 slices fried bread

Heat the oil in a saucepan, reheat the spinach, season with salt and fry briefly, stirring the contents. Add the beaten eggs and grated cheese. Have ready a large saucepan with the boiling broth and transfer the mixture to this. Simmer for a further 5 minutes, then pour into a soup tureen and place the slices of fried bread on the surface before serving.

Previous page The *Tajo* at Ronda, scene of the episode in Hemingway's *For Whom the Bell Tolls*, when Government supporters flung their opponents into the gorge

Top left Maite Manjón and the Spanish cartoonist, Antonio Mingote, look at the lamps used for night fishing at Torre del Mar, near Málaga

Bottom left The former Jewish quarter in Córdoba

Above A *bodega* in the Levante with hanging-metal chains to keep out the flies

Above Cooking a *paella* in the open air

Below Peñiscola, north of Valencia, the last refuge of the Anti-pope, Pedro de Luna

PATATAS CASTELLANAS
POTATOES CASTILIAN STYLE

Serves 6. These potatoes, spiced with paprika, may be served as a starter, as they often are in Castile, or eaten with meat.

4 tablespoons olive oil
1 onion, chopped
1 clove garlic, peeled and chopped
4 lb (2 kg) potatoes, peeled and cut up
1 teaspoon sweet paprika powder
1 tablespoon flour
Salt and pepper
1 bay leaf

Heat the olive oil in a saucepan, fry the chopped onion and garlic until they change colour, then add the potatoes and paprika and continue frying for a little. Sprinkle in the flour and stir with a wooden spoon until the potatoes turn golden. Cover with boiling water, add salt, pepper and the bay leaf and simmer gently for ½ hour.

JUDIAS AL TIO LUCAS
HARICOT BEANS TIO LUCAS

Tío (or 'Uncle') Lucas ran a restaurant in Madrid, which has long since disappeared, but gave his name to a number of dishes, of which this is the best-known.

1 lb (450 g) haricot beans
1 tablespoon olive oil
1 head garlic, peeled
1 bay leaf
White pepper, freshly ground
2 cloves
1 sprig thyme
Salt

If necessary the haricot beans should be left to soak overnight; some types of bean require only an hour or two to soften them.

Put the beans into fresh water in a stewpan. Add all the other ingredients, bring to the boil and cook slowly for 1½ hours. Taste the beans at this point and continue slow cooking for as long as they need to become tender. Check the seasoning and serve in soup plates as a starter.

Buñuelos de bacalao a la espanola
Fish croquettes

These croquettes are somewhere between an ordinary croquette and a soufflé.

3½ oz (100 g) *bacalao* (dried and salted cod)
½ lb (225 g) mashed potato
2 eggs
A little chopped parsley
2 cloves garlic, crushed
3½ oz (100 g) flour
Salt
Nutmeg
Olive oil

The *bacalao* must be soaked overnight. Next morning rinse it thoroughly, remove the skin and bones, and flake it very fine.

Put the freshly-made mashed potato into a bowl and mix it with the flaked *bacalao*, then add the yolks of the two eggs, parsley, garlic, flour, and a little salt and nutmeg. Stir well together, Now beat the whites of the eggs until stiff and fold into the mixture.

Heat some olive oil in a pan. Shape the croquettes with a couple of tablespoons and fry in the hot oil until browned. Place on kitchen paper to remove vestiges of oil and serve piping hot.

Tortilla de patatas a la española
Spanish omelette

Restaurants outside Spain, perhaps in deference to foreign appetites and because it is intended as a starter, often serve up a thin pancake with mixed vegetables embedded in it. The *tortilla* eaten the length and breadth of Spain as a main dish or in cubes as a *tapa* (see page 31) is a thick cake, always containing potatoes and sometimes onion, which makes it juicier.

Olive oil
6 large potatoes, peeled and sliced thin
2 onions, cut into rings
Salt
8 eggs

Heat some olive oil in a pan and fry the mixed potato and onion over a low flame, adding a little salt. It will take about 20 minutes for the potatoes to become sufficiently soft.

Meanwhile beat the eggs in a bowl and add the mixture from the pan with a draining spoon, retaining surplus oil for further use. If the surface of the pan is clean and shiny, it may be used for the next operation; otherwise it must be washed and dried. Put a little of the reserved oil into the pan, heat over a high flame, and when it begins to smoke pour in the egg mixture and cook for 2 or 3 minutes. Now cover the pan with a plate and invert the half-cooked omelette into it. Slide the omelette back into the pan – the uncooked side will now be downwards. Cook for another few minutes. The final result should be golden-brown and about an inch thick, with the inside still juicy. Serve with a green salad as a main dish.

Cocido castellano

Serves 6 to 8. This substantial stew constitutes a complete meal.

12 oz (300 g) chick-peas
Salt
Pinch bicarbonate of soda
1 lb (½ kg) shin of beef, cut up
2 marrow bones
5 oz (150 g) end of ham bone
5 oz (150 g) belly of pork, cut up
1 turnip, cut up
3 leeks, split lengthwise
2 carrots, split lengthwise
2 lb (1 kg) cabbage, washed and cut up
2 tablespoons olive oil
1 clove garlic, chopped
2 oz (60 g) *estrellita* or vermicelli
½ lb (1 kg) potatoes, halved or quartered
5 oz (150 g) *chorizo*

Soak the chick-peas overnight in lukewarm water with a pinch of salt and bicarbonate of soda. Next morning wash them and tie them into a muslin bag, so that they do not disintegrate during cooking.

Put the shin of beef and the marrow and ham bones into a large stewpot with a good quantity of water and bring to the boil over a high flame. Now add the chick-peas in their bag with a little salt. Remove the foam with a spoon and cook gently.

In 1 hour's time add the belly of pork, turnip, leeks and carrots and simmer for another 2 hours; if necessary add a little boiling water to make good what has evaporated.

In a separate saucepan, boil the cabbage in salted water for 15 minutes, drain and reserve.

Heat a little olive oil in a pan, fry the chopped garlic and then add the cabbage, stirring well and finally putting a lid on it to keep it hot.

Half an hour before serving the *cocido*, remove a quantity of broth from the stewpot to make the soup. Transfer it to a saucepan, add the vermicelli (or *estrellita*, which is a fine pasta made especially for this purpose) and cook for 10 minutes.

Meanwhile add the whole potatoes and *chorizo* to the stewpot, cook for 5 minutes, then add the following forcemeat and cook for a further 15 minutes.

Forcemeat for cocidos
3 eggs
3½ oz (100 g) fresh bread, grated
1 tablespoon chopped parsley
1 clove garlic, crushed
Olive oil

Beat the eggs, add the bread, parsley and garlic, and mix well with a wooden spoon. Now shape small flat cakes with the hands and fry them in hot olive oil until golden. Collect them on a plate and add to the stewpot as described.

Serve the different components of the *cocido* separately, as follows:
1. The soup.
2. The chick-peas, taken out of the muslin bag.
3. The vegetables, the potatoes to one side.
4. The meat and forcemeat cakes

Pepitoria de gallina
Chicken with almonds

Olive oil
3 lb (1½ kg) boiling fowl, cut up
Salt
1 onion, chopped
6 walnuts, peeled
8 almonds, blanched in boiling water
2 hard-boiled egg yolks
1 pint (6 dl) chicken broth, made from the giblets or with a cube

Heat a little olive oil in a pan, sprinkle the pieces of chicken with salt, fry until golden and transfer to a stewpot. Using the oil that remains in the pan, fry the chopped onion for about 10 minutes. Drain and add to the chicken in the stewpot. Meanwhile crush the walnuts and almonds in a mortar or mince them with the hard-boiled egg yolks in a 'Mouli'. Add them, together with the chicken broth, and stew gently for 1 hour or until the chicken is tender. Check the seasoning before serving.

Albondigas con salsa rubia
Meatballs in sauce

Meatballs
½ lb (225 g) cooked veal or pork, minced
3½ oz (100 g) cooked ham, minced
1 onion, chopped
Salt
1 egg, beaten
1 dessertspoon fresh breadcrumbs
1 clove garlic, crushed
A little chopped parsley
1½ oz (40 g) flour
Olive oil

Put the minced meat, ham and chopped onion into a bowl and season with salt. Mix thoroughly with the beaten egg, fresh breadcrumbs, garlic and parsley. Shape the balls with your hands, dredge them in flour, then fry for 5 minutes in hot olive oil over a high flame. When golden, remove them with a draining spoon, place on a plate and reserve.

Salsa rubia
1 onion, finely chopped
Olive oil
2 dessertspoons flour
1 small glass dry sherry
¼ pint (150 ml) stock, made with a cube
Salt and pepper

Fry the chopped onion for 10 minutes in hot olive oil, drain off the excess, add the flour and stir in the sherry and broth. Simmer for a few minutes and season with salt and pepper.

Now transfer the sauce to a stewpan, add the meatballs and cook together gently for ½ hour.

Sesos empanados
Crisp fried brains

Sheep's brains (1 per person)
Onion, a few rings
1 carrot
Sprig of parsley
1 bay leaf
1 teaspoon white vinegar
Beaten egg
Flour
Breadcrumbs
Butter for frying

Brains must always be cleaned and pre-cooked, whatever the final method of preparation. To remove the blood, soak the brains in cold water for 20 minutes, then with great care remove the membranes and any small pieces of bone and return the brains to cold water.

Now put them in a saucepan and cover with cold water. Add a few rings of onion, a carrot, a sprig of parsley, a bay leaf and a teaspoon of white vinegar. Bring to the boil, then reduce the heat as low as possible and simmer very gently for about 15 minutes. Drain well and transfer the brains to a bowl, which should be tightly covered to preserve the white colour. When cold they are ready for further use.

Cut the brains into small pieces, dredge them in beaten egg and flour and then in breadcrumbs. Fry slowly in a pan with a little butter until golden.

Sesos a la manteca negra
Brains with 'black' butter

Sheep's brains (1 per person)
Butter
Chopped parsley
2 teaspoons vinegar

The brains must be cleaned, pre-cooked and allowed to cool as described above. Cut them up and put them into a frying pan in which a little butter has been melted, together with chopped parsley. Cook slowly and baste with the butter when they begin to brown. Now stir in two teaspoons of vinegar, allow the liquid to reduce for a minute or two, heat for a further few minutes and serve piping hot.

CHULETAS DE CERDO A LA MADRILEÑA
PORK CHOPS MADRID STYLE

4 pork chops
3 cloves garlic, chopped
A little chopped parsley
2 dessertspoons refined olive oil
1 teaspoon sweet paprika powder
1 bay leaf
A little chopped thyme
Salt and pepper

Put all the ingredients on a glass dish and allow them to marinate for 1 hour, stirring at intervals. Transfer to a stewpan and cook on top of the stove for ¾ hour or a little longer, depending on the thickness of the chops, until browned. Serve with fried potatoes and tomato sauce (see page 52).

CALLOS A LA MADRILEÑA
TRIPE MADRID STYLE

This highly-spiced dish is a world – or country – apart from the bland English tripe and onions.

2 lb (1 kg) tripe, cleaned and cut into strips
1 pig's trotter, blanched
2 tablespoons olive oil
1 onion, chopped
4 oz (120 g) cooked ham, minced
3½ oz (100 g) *chorizo*, chopped
⅔ oz (20 g) tomato purée
2 tablespoons flour
2 chillis, chopped fine
Salt and pepper
Chopped parsley

Tripe must be carefully cleaned before cooking. In England your butcher will already have done this; otherwise proceed as follows.

Cut the tripe into strips and soak in changes of cold water for 4 or 5 hours. Clean the surface with a brush, immerse in a little white vinegar for ½ hour, and soak in further changes of cold water. Now transfer it to a saucepan, cover with cold water and boil for 5 minutes. Remove the froth, throw away the water, and after washing the tripe return it to the saucepan with fresh water, together with a *bouquet garni*, a clove of garlic, an onion and a little salt. Simmer slowly for 2 to 3 hours, after which it is ready for further use.

To cook the cleaned tripe, put it in a stewpan with the pig's trotter, cover with water and cook slowly for an hour, skimming off foam. Remove the pig's trotter with a draining spoon, take out the bones and return the meat to the stewpan.

Heat the olive oil in a pan, fry the chopped onion for about 10 minutes, then add the ham, *chorizo* and tomato purée and cook together for a further few minutes. Now add the flour together with a little of the broth from the tripe, stir well with a wooden spoon and pour the mixture into the stewpan. Add the chillis and a little salt and pepper. Cook together very slowly for 15 minutes and sprinkle with parsley before serving.

Churros

These golden-brown fingers are a favourite for breakfast in Spain and are eaten with coffee or chocolate, in which they are often dunked.

1 pint (½ litre) slightly salted water
14 oz (400 g) sieved flour
2 eggs
Olive oil
Sugar

Bring the water to the boil in a big saucepan over a high heat, add the flour and beat vigorously with a wooden spoon, stirring until the dough no longer sticks to the sides of the pan. Then take the pan from the heat, add the eggs and continue to stir until the paste is completely smooth.

Now fill the dough into a forcing bag, heat some oil in a pan until it smokes and squeeze the mixture into it in dollops shaped like a number 8. Fry the *churros* until they are golden-brown, then remove them with a draining spoon, shake them on kitchen paper to absorb excess oil and put on a serving dish. Powder them with sugar before bringing to the table.

Mazapanes de Toledo
Marzipan

1 lb (½ kg) caster sugar
1 lb (½ kg) almonds

Put the almonds in a bowl and blanch them by pouring in boiling water and then slipping off the skins. Use the blender to shred them, or if you prefer mince them twice in a 'Mouli', so as to obtain fine crumbs. Return this, mixed with the sugar, to the blender or 'Mouli', then moisten your fingers with a little water and work the resulting dough on a pastry board or marble slab.

The paste is now ready to mould into small shapes or figures with the fingers, or it may be pressed into moulds. In Spain these figurines, often made at Christmas time, are painted with a little coloured tragacanth.

Lay them on a metal sheet and bake for a few minutes in a very slow oven until pale yellow.

Pestiños madrileños
A traditional Madrid sweet

4½ oz (125 g) flour
1 oz (30 g) pork fat
Pinch of salt
1 liqueur glass anisette or Pernod
Olive oil

Put the flour in a large bowl and add the pork fat, salt and anisette in that order. Work with the fingers so as to make a smooth paste, if necessary adding a little water. Cover with a clean tea towel and allow to rest for ½ hour. Now roll out the dough as thinly as possible on a pastry board or marble slab and with a pastry cutter divide it into rectangles about 2 × 4 inches (5 × 10 cm).

Heat some olive oil in a pan until it begins to smoke, reduce the heat a little and fry until golden.

Old Castile

Old Castile, the heartland of Spain, extends from north of Madrid across the mountains and as far as Santander on the Atlantic coast. Much of it is barren upland plateau, and that great Spanish philosopher Miguel Unamuno equates the character of its people with the climate, when he writes of the Castilians as 'a race of abstemious men, the product of slow selection by the frosts of the bleakest winters and long periods of destitution, accustomed to a hostile sky and a life of poverty'. The grip of the Moors on the region was never secure; another writer, Pérez Galdós, described their opponents as 'dried beef wrapped in tinder'; and it was from Burgos in the north that El Cid began his one-man campaign against the emirates.

The great and lovely cities which one thinks of as typically Castilian emerged from the repopulation of the area south of the River Duero after Alfonso VI had driven back the Moors. Such are Avila, the mystic city of Santa Teresa with myriad churches, high on a bleak plateau behind its encircling wall; Salamanca, at once the Oxford and Cambridge of Spain; Segovia of the two cathedrals, through which marches the airy Roman aqueduct; and Zamora, still stamped by the treachery that enabled Alfonso VI to become lord of Castile.

Castile did not in fact emerge as a state in her own right until about the time of the Count Garci Fernandez (970-95), and the reoccupation of al-Andalus was achieved with help from the other most powerful kingdom in the Peninsula, Aragon-Catalonia; but when Castile and Aragon were united in 1479 under the Catholic Monarchs, Ferdinand and Isabel, the balance of power tilted irrevocably towards Castile. The conquered territories in America owed their allegiance not to Spain but to its Castilian rulers; and although they were titled 'King of the Spains' and not 'King of Spain', their policies were habitually directed towards the greater glory of Castile.

In gastronomic terms it is sometimes difficult to draw distinctions between Old and New Castile. They share many of the basic ingredients: lamb from the rolling plains, partridge from the mountains, trout from their cold streams (almost every region of Spain claims that *its* trout is the best), the ubiquitous chick-pea and other vegetables in plenty. The *cocido* (see pages 48 and 58) is equally popular in both areas. If one had to name a single type of dish most typical of Old Castile, it would be the roasts of lamb, sucking pig and kid, and for this reason the area is known as the *Zona de los Asados*.

Both Avila and Segovia are renowned for their *cochinillo* (roast sucking pig), prepared from milk-fed piglets smaller than those usually available abroad and cooked in a baker's oven. Although it has sometimes been stigmatized as 'commercial', some of the best sucking pig in Spain may undoubtedly be eaten at the Mesón de Cándido, a small restaurant lying in the shadow of the great Roman aqueduct in Segovia. It is here so tender and succulent that the waiters habitually cut the portions with the edge of a plate. The origins of this venerable establishment go back to the time of Henry IV (1454-74), when a certain Pedro de Cuéllar, a servant of the king's paymaster, lost a leg in his master's service, was pensioned off and opened a hostelry in Segovia, in which he was helped by his wife and daughters. About 1860 the *taberna*, as it now was, was in the hands of the Duque family, who began to specialize in preparing good food, and on the death of Dionisio Duque in 1931 it was taken over by his brother-in-law, Candido Lopez, who consolidated its reputation.

Lechazo or roast milk-fed lamb is perhaps at its best in the north of the region, around Valladolid, where it is also cooked in a baker's oven. One restaurant where it is a speciality is Terete in Haro, situated above its own butcher's shop. Before climbing the homely stairs one passes the old-fashioned brick oven in which the lamb is cooked over an open fire; the scrubbed wooden tables are belied by the excellence of the food; and the visiting Riojan *bodeguero* from one of the town's numerous wineries can be certain of being served his own *reservas*.

Burgos, worth a visit for its fine Gothic cathedral, is known gastronomically both for its dark chocolates, freshly made every day, and for a particularly delicate form of smoked pork chop (*chuleta de cerdo ahumado*), prepared locally but available in restaurants throughout the region.

The roasts of lamb and sucking pig are also excellent in Avila, but the old walled city is particularly well-known for its *yemas de Santa Teresa* (recipe on page 78), a Moorish-inspired sweetmeat akin to the *yemas de San Leandro* from Seville and named in honour of the sixteenth-century mystic, Sta Teresa, who set about her reforms of the Carmelite Order in Avila and more than any one person was responsible for preventing the spread of Protestantism to Spain.

As befits the high tables of its ancient university, Salamanca has a long history of culinary splendour, vividly described by Julián Manuel de Sabando:

> The table is set for, say, eighteen persons, with the finest white porcelain. Each setting is of four plates one above another, a fork, two knives, one large and two small glasses, and a cruet, in addition to polished silver trays and candelabra. In front of each diner is a round wooden box and a large porcelain basin with a lid: the first contains sweetmeats and the second *manjar blanco* [a confection made of rice flour, milk and sugar, sometimes with the addition of minced chicken breasts or ground almonds]. The professors and graduates sit at table and are served by six students chosen for the task. After the preliminaries each diner is served with a roast bird, often turkey . . .

This was a liberal interpretation of the university's statutes, which required that every student offering himself for examination gave to each of his examiners, and also to the doctors and masters of the faculty, a variety of fare including meats, confectionery and three brace of fowl; he was also obliged to entertain them to supper for the whole period of the exams – it is to be hoped that they were not prolonged!

Richard Ford, writing in the 1840s, fills out this description when he describes the dons as:

> siestose men of protruding and pendulous abdomens. . . . Even up to 1747 it was considered a heresy to assert that the sun did not revolve around the earth; so that the capon revolved around the spit, what cared the senior fellows and drony Doctors, contented when not sleeping to suck in the milk of Alma Mater . . .?

The 'milk' most favoured by these men of science was traditionally the strong red wine from the region around Toro, an ancient town further to the north, approached by a Roman bridge and rich in mediaeval churches and seignorial houses with windows barred with heavy metal grilles. The wine, full-bodied and high in alcohol, is known locally as *Sangre de Toro* (bull's blood), but should not be confused either with a proprietary wine of the same name from

Catalonia or that from Hungary. The old proverb:

Tomando vino de Toro
más que comer, devoro;
vino de Toro es oro,
aunque prieto como moro

has it that Toro wine is more for eating than drinking and that, though pure gold, it is as black as a Moor.

The white wines from the *Tierra del Vino*, further east between Toro and Valladolid, are frequently mentioned in Spanish literature from the sixteenth century onwards. Often labelled Rueda, after the name of one of the villages in the area, they grow a *flor* (see page 14), are golden in colour and long-lived, and not surprisingly have a taste reminiscent of sherry. A good place to try them is in the bars of the neighbouring university city of Valladolid, where they are served from the cask under the name of 'Serrada'.

The major producer of fine Spanish table wines, the Rioja, lies on the northern fringe of Old Castile, but it was historically part of Navarra, with which it is more closely linked, and is described in the following chapter.

There remains one red wine from Old Castile, which is considered by its admirers, among whom was Winston Churchill who tasted it at a banquet at the Spanish Embassy, to be the best in Spain. The estate of Vega Sicilia lies some forty kilometres to the east of Valladolid on the border of the River Duero. After the damaging phylloxera epidemic, its vineyards were replanted with Bordeaux grapes grafted on to resistant American stocks. The wine is now made from a mixture of the original French grapes, propagated in the bodega's nurseries, together with native growths, including a little of the white Albillo. Only the juice from the first pressing of the grapes is used, and it is fermented very slowly and aged for long periods in 225-litre casks similar to those used in Bordeaux. Only wine aged for ten years or more is sold as Vega Sicilia, the rest being labelled 'Valbuena'. Production is strictly limited, and Vega Sicilia is an expensive wine by any standards, supplies being rationed to a limited number of the best Spanish restaurants – including, in Madrid, Valentín, Mayte Commodore and that of the Ritz Hotel – and some of the Paradores. A small amount is now being shipped to England by those specialists in fine Spanish wines, Laymont and Shaw of Falmouth.

The wines are full-bodied, fruity and heady to a degree, often containing some 15 or 16 per cent of alcohol. A doyen of the London wine trade once made the interesting comment that their flavour reminded him of port and ventured the opinion, interesting since both wines are grown in the same river valley, that they had been made with Douro grapes fermented to completion without being brandied.

As a tailpiece, Old Castile makes some whisky. The distillery was set up at Segovia with guidance from Scottish technicians, but be warned! Its product, widely sold in Spain as 'D.Y.C.', bears little resemblance to the original.

Recipes

Ancas de rana rebozadas
Fried frogs' legs

2 dozen frogs' legs
Salt and pepper
Flour
3 eggs, beaten
Olive oil or pork fat for frying
1 sprig parsley

It is usual to buy frogs' legs ready for cooking, otherwise they must be cleaned. First skewer the legs, then skin them and immerse them in water, changing it every hour or so until the meat is tender and white. They are now ready for cooking.

Dry the legs and season them with salt and pepper. Now dredge them in flour, shake off the excess and dip them in beaten egg. Fry in hot olive oil or fat until golden, decorate with parsley and serve very hot.

Pescado a medio escabeche
Marinated fish

This is served as a starter. The quantity of olive oil and other ingredients for the marinade depends upon the size of the vessel used.

Olive oil, 4 parts
Vinegar, 2 parts
Lemon juice, 1 part
1 sprig of parsley
1 bay leaf
1 lb (½ kg) firm white fish
Green olives

Prepare the marinade with the first five ingredients as if making a vinaigrette sauce. Meanwhile clean and skin the fish and cut it into slices. Cover the fish with the sauce and simmer for some 15 minutes (depending on its thickness). Allow it to cool and leave in the sauce for 3 hours, then remove the bones and arrange on a serving dish surrounded by the olives. Serve with tartare or other sauce appropriate for fish.

Lentejas zamoranas
Lentils Zamora style

A rib-warming stew, best served on a cold winter's evening.

1 lb (½ kg) lentils, soaked overnight
1 onion, chopped
2 cloves garlic, one crushed, the other whole
3 *morcillas* (blood sausage) or black pudding
Olive oil
1 tablespoon sweet paprika powder
1 sprig of parsley
Salt

To 3½ pints (2 litres) of cold water in a stewpan, add the lentils, chopped onion, the whole clove of garlic and the *morcillas*. Bring to the boil and simmer slowly.

Now heat a little olive oil in a pan and fry the chopped garlic very briefly until it changes colour. Remove from the fire and stir in the paprika powder and then add to the stewpan with the parsley and cook the lentils for about 1 hour or until tender. Season with salt halfway through cooking.

Arroz a la santanderina
Rice Santander style

If served with poached eggs, this makes a good supper dish.

4 teacups rice
6 teacups water
2 oz (50 g) butter
Salt
2 teacups milk
7 oz (200 g) ham, diced

Boil the rice in the water for ten minutes or until the water has evaporated. Now add half the butter, a little salt, the milk and ham and simmer for another 5 minutes (the total cooking time should be about 20 minutes). Once all the liquid has been absorbed, add the rest of the butter and bake in a fireproof dish in a moderate oven (350° / 180° C/ Mark 4) until the rice is browned. It should be ready in about 10 or 15 minutes.

Pisto castellano

A vegetable dish, rather resembling *ratatouille*, which may be eaten either as a starter or with a main course.

2 oz (60 g) pork fat
3 onions, chopped
2 oz (60 g) belly of pork or streaky bacon, cut fine
1 lb (½ kg) courgettes, peeled and cut up
3 medium-sized potatoes, peeled and sliced
4 red peppers, fresh and deseeded or from a can, cut into strips
4 tomatoes, blanched and skinned
2 eggs, beaten
Salt and pepper

Heat the pork fat in a pan, fry the chopped onions for 5 minutes, then add the belly of pork or bacon and fry together for another 5 minutes. Now add the courgettes, potatoes, peppers and tomatoes and simmer for ¾ hour, taking care that the mixture does not dry out. If necessary, add a little broth made from a bouillon cube.

Stir in the beaten eggs, season with salt and pepper, and stir with a wooden spoon until the egg is cooked.

When prepared as a main dish, the *pisto* may be served with fried bread.

Cachelada leonesa
Potatoes with spiced sausage

In the uplands of León, where this warming dish is a favourite in winter, it is made with the local *chorizo* (see page 161), which comes in sausages of about ½ lb (225 g).

2 lb (1 kg) large potatoes
2 *chorizos*
Salt

Choose large, sound potatoes, peel them and cut them into two or three. Now put them into a stewpot with the *chorizos*, cover them with water and season with salt. Cook for 20 minutes, then drain off the water (which may be used for soup) and serve the potatoes – which with their red colour look as spicy as they taste – flanked by the *chorizos.*

Codornices a la casera
Quail country style

2 cleaned quail
2 oz (60 g) pork fat
2 oz (60 g) belly of pork, cut into strips
2 oz (60 g) cooked ham, cut into strips
6 shallots
2 oz (60 g) mushrooms
1 teaspoon mixed herbs
Salt and pepper
1 large glass dry white wine
1 large cup broth

Put the quail into a roasting tin surrounded by the other ingredients and pour over them the wine and broth. Sauté briefly on top of the stove, then bake in a preheated oven (350° F/180° C/Mark 4) for 20 minutes to ½ hour, basting at intervals.

Codornices al nido
Quail in nest

2 cleaned quail
½ lb (225 g) belly of pork, cut into strips
4 oz (110 g) pork fat
Salt and pepper
Straw potatoes

Proceed as if roasting a chicken. Put the quail in a roasting tin and cover the breasts with the strips of pork. Melt the fat and pour it on top, season with salt and freshly-ground pepper, then roast in a preheated oven (350° F/180° C/Mark 4) for 20 minutes to ½ hour.

Serve in a nest of straw potatoes.

Perdices estofadas con chocolate
Stewed partridge with chocolate

Serves 2. This intriguing recipe for cooking partridge with chocolate, also typical of Navarra, possibly dates from the introduction of cocoa beans to Spain from South America.

2 partridge of 1 lb (½ kg) or 1 of 2 lb (1 kg)
1 onion, cut up
1 head of garlic, whole
1 clove
1 bay leaf
A little olive oil
1½ teacups dry white wine
½ teacup vinegar
Salt and pepper
1 oz (30 g) cooking chocolate

Put the partridge in a stewpot, together with the cut-up onion and the head of garlic with a clove inserted in it. Add the bay leaf, olive oil, wine, vinegar and a little salt and pepper, bring to the boil and simmer for ¾ to 1 hour (the time varies according to whether there are two small partridge or one large one), shaking the pot at intervals.

Now remove the partridge and place on a serving dish. Meanwhile add the grated chocolate to the contents of the stewpot, cook with the other ingredients for a further 10 minutes, then rub the sauce through a sieve with a wooden spoon and pour it on top of the partridge.

Serve with slices of fried potato, which should be arranged around the partridge before the sauce is poured on, so that it covers the whole dish.

Perdices estofadas
Stewed partridge
Serves 2.

2 partridge, cleaned and prepared
A little olive oil
A little pork fat
5 oz (150 g) ham, diced
2 cloves garlic, chopped
1 bay leaf
Pinch of thyme
Salt and pepper
Cinnamon
1 glass dry white wine

Brown the partridge in the mixed olive oil and pork fat and transfer to a stewpot. Using the same pan and oil, fry the chopped ham for about 5 minutes, then add the chopped garlic, the bay leaf and thyme. Stir together and pour over the partridge, seasoning with salt and pepper and a pinch of cinnamon. Pour in the wine and cook gently for about ½ hour, depending on the size of the birds, until they are tender.

Sesos bandera española
Brains with mayonnaise

This makes an attractive starter. *Bandera* means a flag; and the dish is so-called because the ingredients, laid alternately on the serving dish, make up the yellow and red of the Spanish colours.

Sheep's brains (1 per person)
1 red pepper, cooked, deseeded and cut into strips (see page 22) or 1 canned pepper
Mayonnaise (see page 116)
Gherkins
Capers

Cook the brains as described on page 61, leave them to cool, then arrange them on a serving dish, pouring on a little mayonnaise. Place the strips of peppers between the brains, so as to make the bands of the 'flag'. Garnish around the outside with gherkins and capers.

Cordero asado al estilo de Castilla
Roast baby lamb Castilian style
Serves 6 or 7.

½ baby lamb (*lechazo*)
Salt and pepper
½ glass dry white wine

Season the lamb with salt and pepper and put it in a roasting tin with the wine. Bake in a hot oven (400° F / 200° C / Mark 6) for 20 minutes, then reduce the temperature fo 250° F / 180° C / Mark 4 for the remainder of the time, taking a total of 15-20 minutes per lb (½ kg) until the lamb is browned on the outside. Baste from time to time with the juice from the meat.

Serve with potato purée or fried potatoes.

Pierna de cabrito asada
Roast leg of kid
This recipe is also suitable for leg of lamb.

1 leg of kid or lamb
1 or 2 cloves of garlic, peeled
Salt
2 oz (60 g) butter, pork fat or olive oil
1 small glass brandy

Put the leg into a roasting tin, rub it with the garlic, season with salt and moisten with the olive oil or daub the fat on top. Roast in a preheated oven (375° F/190° C/Mark 5) for 20 minutes per lb (½ kg). Halfway through cooking, pour the glass of brandy over the roast, which will give it a rich colour and improve the flavour.

When the meat is done, place it on a serving dish and keep it hot in the oven. Meanwhile skim off the fat from the juices in the roasting tin, add a little white wine and stir well with a wooden spoon to make a gravy for serving with the roast.

COCHINILLO ASADO
ROAST SUCKING PIG

Serves 8–10. A dish for an occasion, such as Christmas. The sucking pig will already have been opened and cleaned by the butcher; it may be plain-roasted or stuffed.

A traditional Spanish stuffing

4 oz (100 g) sausagemeat
8 oz (225 g) cooked ham, chopped
Liver from the piglet, chopped
8 oz (225 g) mushrooms, chopped
6 shallots, chopped
2 eggs, beaten
4 oz (110 g) fresh breadcrumbs
1 tablespoon parsley, chopped
Salt and pepper
1 teaspoon mixed herbs
1 small glass *aguardiente* (see page 147) or brandy
Olive oil

Mix together all the ingredients except the olive oil, fill the cavity of the piglet with the stuffing and sew up with a strong needle and thread. Smear the outside with olive oil and coarse salt and place on an oven rack in the roasting tin.

If unstuffed, the piglet should be rubbed with oil and salt, opened and placed on the oven rack. Pieces of foil around the mouth and ears will prevent them from blackening.

Preheat the oven to 375° F/190° C/Mark 5, and roast an 8–10 lb (3½–4½ kg) sucking pig for 2 hours 15 minutes to 2 hours 45 minutes, with an additional ¼ hour at 425° F/220° C/Mark 7, to crisp the outside. Garnish with an apple in the mouth.

It is something of an undertaking to roast a sucking pig – when ordering from the butcher, make sure that your oven is large enough to take it.

TORTILLA AZUCARADA
SWEET OMELETTE

Since these omelettes are light and fluffy they are best made individually, rather than as a large omelette to serve several people.

2 eggs
Caster sugar
Grated lemon peel
A little butter

Separate the yolks from the whites of the eggs. Beat a little caster sugar and grated lemon peel into the yolks, and beat the whites until stiff. Blend the egg mixtures, then heat a little butter in an omelette pan. Cook like a French omelette on one side only, finally folding it over and serving it with all speed.

LECHE FRITA
'FRIED MILK'

A popular sweet in Old Castile.

4 eggs
4 tablespoons flour
4 tablespoons caster sugar
½ pint (3 dl) milk
1 stick cinnamon
Knob of butter
Flour for coating
Olive oil for frying

Beat two of the eggs, pour into a saucepan and add the flour, sugar, milk, cinnamon stick and knob of butter. Stir well together, then simmer over a low fire, continuing to stir until the mixture is thick. Grease a large dish with butter, spread out the dough and allow it to cool.

Now cut it into strips or other shapes, dredge them in the other two beaten eggs and flour, then fry in smoking hot olive oil until browned. (They may be fried either in deep or shallow oil; if using shallow oil, turn them over once.) Powder with extra caster sugar, arrange on a serving dish and bring to the table without delay.

Tocino de cielo

This dish, which we have seen translated in Spanish menus as 'Salt Pork Sky' (!), is in fact another favourite sweet.

12 eggs
1 lb (450 g) caster sugar
9 fl. oz (25 cl) water
1 vanilla pod

Break the eggs and pass them through a sieve. Heat 12 oz (340 g) of the sugar in the water with the vanilla pod until it forms 'ropy' strands when a spoon is dipped into the liquid and the syrup is allowed to drip back. Incorporate the syrup with the egg mixture, little by little and stirring continuously. Make a little caramel by heating the remaining 4 oz (110 g) of sugar with a teaspoon of water until dark in colour, and with this coat a mould. Pour in the mixture of egg and syrup and cook in a *bain-marie* or large saucepan of boiling water for 10 minutes, covering the mould with foil so as to prevent the water splashing into it. Allow to cool, then turn out the contents of the mould on to a serving dish.

Yemas de Santa Teresa
Yolks of Santa Teresa

3 oz (90 g) caster sugar
2½ fl. oz (75 ml) water
½ cinnamon stick
1 twist lemon peel
6 egg yolks
A little icing sugar

Stir the sugar, water, cinnamon and lemon peel in a saucepan and simmer until the liquid forms viscous strands. Put the egg yolks in another saucepan, add the syrup and stir well. Cook over a slow fire, stirring all the time, until the paste no longer sticks to the side of the pan. Turn out on to a dish and allow to cool. Sprinkle with icing sugar, cut into twelve portions and serve in paper cases.

Aragon and Navarra

The Kingdom of Navarra, lying between the French frontier and Catalonia to the extreme north-west of Spain, and that of Aragon, bordering it on the south, are closely linked in terms of gastronomy.

Both played their part in the early days of the Reconquest of the country from the Moors. The fortunes of Aragon reached a zenith under Alfonso *el Batallador*, ('the Battler', 1073-1134), who reoccupied most of the Ebro basin and struck deep into al-Andalus, although he was unable to achieve his objective of capturing Granada from the Moors. In the words of the chronicler Ibn al-Athir, 'No Christian prince was more valorous than he or possessed of such ardour for fighting the Muslims or of such powers of resistance. . . . With his death Allah allowed the faithful to breathe again, free from his hammer blows.' Shortly after his death, the shrewd Ramon Berenguer IV of Barcelona succeeded in uniting Aragon and Catalonia by marrying Alfonso's grand-daughter, the Infanta Petronila; and thereafter the fortunes of the two states were linked under the Crown of Aragon, controlled by the Counts of Barcelona. Nevertheless, when the dynasty expired on the death of Martin the Humane in 1410, it was the Aragonese, who, by opting for the Castilian Ferdinand of Antequera, brought the eventual union of Spain within reach.

Centring on Pamplona, Navarra at one time extended across the Pyrenees into France; hence the alternative spelling of 'Navarre' and its many gastronomic links with Béarn. The small Basque state, hemmed in as it was by more powerful neighbours, was unable to expand at the expense of the Moors and became fair game for the territorial ambitions of Castile, the Crown of Aragon and France. Successive rulers prolonged its existence by exploiting the differences between the bordering states; but in 1512 it fell to Ferdinand the Catholic and it was then incorporated in Castile, the area across the Pyrenees going to France.

The mountain regions of both Aragon and Navarra are famous for their lamb. In Aragon it may be roasted or served as the picturesquely-named *esparragos montañeses* ('mountain asparagus') – in fact the lambs' tails, stewed and served in a sauce of tomatoes and peppers. Equally well-known in Navarra is the tender young *cochifrito*, cut up and cooked with onion, garlic, peppers, parsley and lemon juice (see page 93) and the *chuletas de cordero a la Navarra*, lamb chops served with a sauce prepared by frying onion and tomato with ham and garnished with *chorizo* (page 94). Aragon is often labelled the '*Zona de los Chilindrónes*', in recognition of another famous sauce, which may accompany either chicken or lamb (see page 92).

Migas or savoury fried breadcrumbs (see page 88) are popular all over Spain and are sometimes said to predate the invasions of classical times and to be an Iberian survival. Particularly associated with Aragon, they are humble enough peasant fare, but are reputed to have been the favourite not only of El Cid, but of James the Conqueror and the ill-starred Lovers of Teruel.

Saragossa, the capital of Aragon and the site of the great cathedral, with its cult of the Virgen del Pilar, has always been renowned for its cuisine, which includes such delicacies as *lomo de cerdo a la zaragozana* (loin of pork in its special sauce), *angulas con judías* (freshwater eels) and *bacalao zaragozano* (dried salt cod). If you drive south from Saragossa to Teruel, you will pass mile upon mile of gardens and orchards, which produce some of the most luscious fruit in Spain, including peaches, plums, apricots, apples, cherries and strawberries.

The vegetables are no less excellent; and one salad, prescribed by his doctor for the ailing Martin the Humane, has found its way into the pages of Spanish – not to say, medical – history. It was made very simply by making four criss-cross cuts in a raw white Aragonese cabbage and inserting into the cuts leaves of the curly cardoon (a species of edible thistle). Conrado Solsona, who unearthed the story, goes on to explain:

> The good king of Aragon ate the salad every night, but as the years passed and his lymph accumulated, the royal doctor ordered a modified diet to alleviate his complaint. All dishes containing gelatin, fats and syrups were eliminated and replaced by those rich in protein and roughage.
>
> Even the salad came under review, and while the cabbage and cardoon were retained, they were augmented with lettuce leaves, reputedly rich in protein. It is for this reason that the saying goes that lettuce 'makes blood' . . .

There is a refrain current in Aragon,which almost certainly echoes the words of Don Martin's doctor: 'Between cabbage and cabbage . . . lettuce.'

Apart from making some excellent cheeses, like that of Roncal, which Rubert de Nola (see page 4) eulogizes in his *Llibre de Coch* as being as 'good and buttery as the best from Italy', Navarra has other culinary contributions to its credit. A vegetable soup, known as *garbure* and made from potatoes, cabbage, green beans, broad beans, peas, belly of pork, loin of pork, sausages and ham bones, is equally renowned in Béarn, the other side of the Pyrenees, where it is made in somewhat different fashion. The intriguing partridge with chocolate has already been mentioned in connection with Old Castile (page 73).

It seems justifiable on historical and ethnic grounds to describe the Rioja in connection with Navarra rather than Castile, and the region produces the best range of table wines in the country. (The Rioja was, in fact, part of Navarra until it fell to Alfonso VIII of Castile in 1180. The monastery of Santa María at Nájera, on the southern border of the Rioja, with the serried tombs of the monarchs of Navarra, bears eloquent testimony to its old allegiance; and even today the commercial ties of the bodegas are principally with Bilbao to the north, while the Sunday trippers who flood into the wine towns to fill their carafes are from Santander, Bilbao and San Sebastián.)

To deal with the lesser wines first, Aragon produces a great deal of wine for everyday drinking. It was formerly fermented in underground cisterns, possibly of Phoenician origin, but is now very largely made in the cement vats of the large cooperatives. Production centres on Cariñena, south-east of Saragossa; and its strong and heady wines, mostly red and often containing as much as 17° or 18° of alcohol, are marketed all over the country; they are also much in demand for blending.

The best of the Navarre wines are grown around Puente de la Reina, an historic old town just south of Pamplona on the pilgrim route from France to Santiago de Compostela. Those to seek out – and they are obtainable at good hotels and the local Paradores, notably that at Olite, installed in the former palace of the Kings of Navarre – are from the Vinícola Navarra and the Señorío de Sarriá. The winery at the Señorio is unlike any other in Spain. It was started in 1952 by the wealthy Huarte Beaumont family as part of a model estate, which also extends to orchards and a stock-raising establishment, and no trouble is spared to produce wines of the best possible quality. All the grapes are grown on the estate; the wines are matured in casks of Armagnac oak made in the bodega's own coopery; and with a capacity of six thousand 225-litre *barricas*, output is very sizable. Even the youngest of the red wines, the 'Ecoyen', is aged for three to four years in wood and another six months in bottle, while the 'Gran Vino de Señorio Reserva' spends some twelve years in cask and two in bottle. It emerges fruity, full-bodied and with a deep bouquet. The bodega also makes white and rosé wines.

The Rioja is more or less synonymous with fine Spanish table wines and its history has already been described (see page 8). The region certainly deserves a visit on any gastronomic tour of Spain and since it is compact, extending for about 100 km along the Ebro valley from Haro in the west to Alfaro in the east (of which only the western half produces the best wine), one may explore it from Logroño, where there are two excellent hotels, the modern and luxurious Carlton Rioja and the more traditional Gran Hotel; from the atmospheric Paradero of Samaniego installed in an old baronial house in the mediaeval walled town of Laguardia; or from the Parador at Santo Domingo de la Calzada, even more interesting historically, since it was once a hospice for pilgrims on their way to the shrine of St James at Santiago de Compostela. In the cathedral adjoining the Parador, there is what must be one of the strangest features in *any* church: a monument to Santo Domingo embodying a cage occupied by a live cock and hen. Just why, you must enquire on the spot!

The Rioja vineyards extend for some 20 km on each side of the River Ebro and the best are in the northerly regions of La Rioja Alta and Rioja Alavesa. The vines are grown low without supporting wires, and six main types of grape are used: for the red wines, the Garnacho, Tempranillo, Graciano and Mazuelo; and for the whites, the Malvasia and Viura. As against the hundred of châteaux and domaines in the classical wine-growing districts of France, there are only some fifty large bodegas entitled to export wines with the *Denominacion de Origen* (correponding to the French *Appellation Controlée*). Some of them maintain their own vineyards, but all buy additional grapes from local farmers. The larger establishments, such as the Bodegas Bilbaínas, Santiago and Franco Españolas, welcome visits to their wineries without special appointment and are centred in Logroño, around Haro in the north and in the townships of Fuenmayor and Cenicero.

Red Riojas differ from comparable French wines by being aged for much longer periods in wood – even the youngest wines must spend two years in oak to qualify for the *Denominación de Origen*, while the *reservas* are matured for upwards of six years before being bottled – and this results in the characteristic flavour, sometimes described as vanilla-like. In the new bodegas now springing up with the backing of the large banks and sherry firms, there is more emphasis on bottle age. While the Rioja is best-known for its dry, full-bodied red wines, the region also produces some excellent dry white wines, best drunk when fairly young, when they may approach Rhône wine standards, also sweet white wines and even some good sparkling wine (the 'Royal Carlton' from the Bodegas Bilbainas, made by the champagne method in its deep cellars).

There is no official classification of the growths of the Rioja, but the two bodegas which have always commanded the highest prices for their wines are the Marqués de Murrieta and the Marqués de Riscal. Murrieta makes exceptionally fruity reds – its *reservas*, like the Castillo Ygay, are outstanding – and a dry white, again full of flavour. The reds from Riscal are lighter, more approaching claret in style. The bodega also makes a good rosé and also a white made with grapes from outside the region.

In general, any wine carrying the seal of the Consejo Regulador (*Denominación de Origen*) may be bought with confidence. The bottles are usually labelled, not with the year of vintage, but according to the time that the wine has spent in cask; thus 4° Año means that it was bottled during the fourth year after the harvest. In terms of quality and price they fall into three broad categories: inexpensive 2° Año or 3° Año wines; wines of up to 6° Año; and old reserves, which often carry the year of vintage. Some of these last, such as those from the Bodegas Bilbaínas; La Rioja Alta; López de Heredia, Viña Tondonia S.A.; Bodegas Riojanas; Compañía Vinícola del Norte de España (CUNE) – to mention only a few – are very fine.

The following vocabulary, reproduced from *The Wines of Spain and Portugal* (Faber, 1973) by Jan Read, in which the interested reader will find more detailed information, will perhaps be helpful in making a choice from a Spanish wine list:

Tinto: Full-bodied red
Clarete: Light red
Rosado: Rosé
Blanco: White
Espumoso: Sparkling
Reserva: Mature wine of good quality. Reserva 1964 refers to wine set aside to mature in that year
Vino de mesa, Vino de pasta: Table wine
Sangría: Red wine containing citrus fruit. Best made with fresh fruit (see page 100), but now bottled

Abocado, Dulce: Sweet
Seco: Dry
4° Año: Bottled in the fourth year after the harvest
Cosecha, Vendímia: Vintage, e.g. Cosecha 1955
Viña, Viñedo: Vineyard. Used rather loosely. Viña Vial does *not* mean that the wine originated exclusively from a vineyard of that name
Cepa: Literally, a 'vine'. Its use on labels is not precise, though the word is sometimes coupled with the name of a grape
Embotellado por: Bottled by
Criado por, Elaborado por: Matured and/or blended by
Añejo, añejado por: Old, aged by
Bodega: Literally, a wine cellar, but used to describe a concern which may have grown, made, shipped or sold the wine. Without further qualification it normally means that the bodega has made and shipped the wine
Denominación de Origen: The guarantee of the Consejo Regulador. All genuine Rioja carries the seal on the label in the form of a small facsimile stamp

Recipes

SALSA ARAGONESA
ARAGONESE SAUCE

This is served cold with fish, eggs, or vegetables.

1 tablespoon water
1 teaspoon lemon juice
2 egg yolks
7 fl. oz (2 dl) olive oil
Salt

Put the water, lemon juice and yolks into a small saucepan and cook over a slow fire, stirring with a wooden spoon until they form a smooth cream. Remove from the fire and add the olive oil little by little, stirring continuously as if making mayonnaise. If the sauce is too thick, add a teaspoon of cold water. Season to taste with salt.

Garbure
A vegetable soup from Navarra

Although this rich broth and the well-known *Garbure Béarnais* from the other side of the Pyrenees are of common origin, the Spanish version differs from the French in that the meat is served with the other ingredients.

2½ pints (1½ litres) meat broth
9 oz (250 g) broad beans, shelled
9 oz (250 g) garden peas, shelled
4 potatoes, peeled and cut up
9 oz (250 g) green beans, cut up
8 oz (225 g) spring greens or cabbage, cut up
3½ oz (100 g) fresh belly of pork, cut up
3½ oz (100 g) loin of pork, in one piece
4 sausages
1 ham bone
Salt

Put the meat broth, if available, into a stewpot; otherwise use water and a cube. Bring to the boil, then add the other ingredients and season with salt. Simmer for 1½ hours and serve very hot.

Coliflor al ajo arriero
Cauliflower country style

This may be served as a starter or with roasts.

1 cauliflower
Salt
2 cloves garlic
1 tablespoon chopped parsley
A little olive oil
1 dessertspoon sweet paprika powder
1 dessertspoon white vinegar

Wash the cauliflower and cut off the outside leaves, then boil it for 15–20 minutes in salted water – without using a lid, so as to retain the white colour. Meanwhile crush one of the cloves of garlic with the parsley in a mortar. Cut up the other and fry it briefly in hot olive oil without allowing it to blacken. Remove the pan from the fire, add the paprika and vinegar and reduce for a minute or two, then stir in the paste of garlic and parsley. Drain the cauliflower, pour the sauce over it and serve hot.

Menestra de Tudela

A mixed vegetable dish from Tudela

Eaten as a starter in Spain, it is nevertheless nourishing enough for a supper dish.

7 oz (200 g) broad beans, shelled
7 oz (200 g) garden peas, shelled
A little olive oil
1 onion, cut up
2 oz (60 g) green bacon, cut up
2 oz (60 g) ham, cut up
2 bay leaves
1 glass light red Rioja
2 large tomatoes, blanched and skinned
1 clove garlic
1 small packet saffron
White pepper, freshly ground
Salt
2 hard-boiled eggs, sliced

Boil the beans and peas separately for 15 minutes (to avoid discolouration), drain and reserve. Now heat the olive oil in a pan and fry the chopped onion for about 10 minutes with the green bacon, chopped ham and bay leaves. Pour in the wine, allow to reduce a little, then stir in the tomatoes with a wooden spoon until they are completely broken up. Add the cooked beans and peas and mix well with the spoon.

Meanwhile pound the garlic, saffron and pepper in a mortar, stir with a teaspoon of water and add to the vegetables. Season with salt and cook over a low fire for 10 minutes, taking care that the mixture does not stick to the pan (add a little more water if necessary). Serve hot on a dish decorated with the slices of hard-boiled egg.

The Ministry of Tourism's *hostería* at Alcalá de Henares, once part of the old university and now a favourite restaurant for Madrileños

Above A typical village in La Mancha. The donkeys with their *alforjas* were formerly the main means of transport

Below The chalky vineyards of Vega Sicilia, near Valladolid

The winery at Vega Sicilia, which produces one of the choicest Spanish red wines

A shepherd and his dog in the uplands of Aragon. At midday, in the shade of a tree, he will eat a home-made *tortilla* and refresh himself from his leather *bota*

Pimientos rellenos a la riojana
Stuffed peppers Rioja style

A piquant variant on the more familiar method of stuffing peppers with rice.

1 lb (½ kg) minced pork
4 eggs
Pinch of nutmeg
1 clove garlic, crushed
A little chopped parsley
Pinch of freshly ground pepper
Salt
8 red peppers, deseeded and baked, or the equivalent from a can
Flour
Olive oil
2 onions, chopped
1 teaspoon sweet paprika powder
½ pint (3 dl) water, or broth if available

Mix the minced pork in a bowl with two of the beaten eggs, the nutmeg, garlic, parsley and a little pepper and salt. If the peppers are fresh, remove the capsules and seeds, and if from a can open them carefully with your fingers (canned peppers can only be stuffed if they are whole, as are those actually canned in Spain; some Spanish peppers canned in England are split). Fill the cavity with the stuffing and secure the top with a cocktail stick. Now dredge the filled peppers in the other two beaten eggs and flour and fry them in hot olive oil. If you have it, use an earthenware *cazuela* large enough to avoid putting the peppers on top of one another.

Remove and reserve the peppers, and in the remaining oil fry the chopped onions for 15 minutes, then add the paprika powder, a dessertspoon of flour and the broth or water. Simmer the sauce for 5 minutes, then ladle it on top of the peppers and cook very slowly for another ½ hour or a little longer if using fresh peppers.

Migas al estilo de Teruel
Savoury breadcrumbs from Teruel

A traditional recipe from Aragon, where these breadcrumbs often form part of an early lunch or are served as a starter to the evening meal. Some devotees even eat them with hot chocolate or with grapes, and they may obviously be served on the side with a variety of main dishes.

9 oz (250 g) stale bread
Salt
Olive oil
2 cloves garlic

Cut the bread into fingers, including the crust. Moisten a napkin with water, sprinkle it with salt, then wrap up the bread and leave it overnight.

Now heat a little olive oil in a pan and fry the whole cloves of garlic until they are on the point of blackening. At this stage remove and discard them, then add the moist bread, stirring energetically with a palette knife to break it up. Fry for 10 minutes and serve hot from the pan.

Huevos al plato a la Navarra
Baked eggs Navarre style

A little butter or olive oil
4 tomatoes, blanched and skinned
A little chopped parsley
Salt and pepper
8 eggs
8 slices *chorizo* from Pamplona
2 oz (60 g) grated Parmesan or Cheddar cheese

Put a little olive oil or butter into small individual *cazuelas* or fireproof dishes. Shred a tomato into each of them, sprinkle with parsley, season with salt and pepper and fry for a few minutes.

Now break two eggs into each *cazuela*, arrange the slices of *chorizo* around the outside, sprinkle with grated cheese and bake in a slow oven until the whites are set, while the yolks remain soft.

Bacalao en salsa verde al estilo de Navarra
Bacalao in green sauce Navarre style

Dried and salted cod is popular even in places removed from the sea, and every region has its own way of cooking it.

2 lb (1 kg) *bacalao* (dried and salted cod)
1 lb (½ kg) cooked green peas
A little olive oil
1 onion, chopped
2 cloves garlic, chopped
Salt

Soak the *bacalao* in cold water overnight. Change the water the following morning, rinse the fish well, then remove the skin and bones and reserve on a plate. Make a purée of the peas, if possible while they are still hot, by rubbing them through a sieve. Heat the olive oil in a pan or *cazuela*, fry the chopped onion for about 10 minutes, then add the chopped garlic and flaked *bacalao*, stirring well with a wooden spoon. Cook gently until the *bacalao* has lost the soaked-up water, stir in the purée of peas and a little salt, and allow another 10 minutes' slow cooking. Serve hot from the fire.

Bacalao a la riojana
Bacalao Rioja style

Another way of cooking *bacalao* from the wine region of the Rioja.

2 lb (1 kg) *bacalao* (dried and salted cod)
Olive oil
2 onions, cut up
1 clove garlic, chopped
4 oz (110 g) canned red peppers, cut into strips
1 dessertspoon sweet paprika powder

Choose thick slices of *bacalao* from the middle of the fish for this dish. Soak them in cold water overnight and in further changes of water next morning. Remove, drain and skin the fish, then open it carefully so that it does not disintegrate, to take out the backbone. Reserve on a plate.

Heat a little olive oil in a pan and fry the chopped onion and garlic slowly for some 10 minutes, so that they soften without turning colour.

Now place a layer of *bacalao* in an oven dish, cover it with some of the fried onion, strips of pimiento and a sprinkling of paprika. Add further layers in the same manner until all the ingredients are used up. Bring to the boil on top of the stove, then bake in a moderate oven (350° F/180° C/Mark 4) for 20 minutes.

Besugo al arriero
Sea bream country style

Fish
1 bream of 2–3 lb (1–1½ kg)
Salt
1 onion
Sprig of parsley
1 dessertspoon vinegar

Clean, wash and dry the bream, then put it in a fish pan with a little water and salt; the onion, cut in halves; the sprig of parsley; and the vinegar. Simmer slowly for 20 minutes or alternatively wrap the fish and other ingredients (but without addition of water) in cooking foil and bake it in a very moderate oven (325° F/ 170° C/Mark 3) for 20 minutes. Now remove the fish and put it on a hot plate, reserving the liquid in which it cooked.

Sauce

1 little olive oil
1 clove garlic
1 dessertspoon flour
1 heaped teaspoon sweet paprika powder
1 teaspoon white vinegar
½ teacup stock, from cooking the fish

Heat a little olive oil in a pan, fry the clove of garlic until golden, then remove and discard it. Stir the flour into the oil and cook it with the paprika, vinegar and stock, so as to make a sauce. Season with salt and pour over the bream. Serve with slices of lemon.

ATUN CON CEBOLLA
TUNA WITH ONION

Serves 2.

9 oz (250 g) tomatoes, blanched, peeled and chopped
5 oz (150 g) onions, finely chopped
2 cloves garlic, chopped
1 tablespoon parsley, chopped
1 oz (25 g) ground walnuts
3 or 4 tablespoons olive oil
1 lb (½ kg) boned tuna fillets
Salt and pepper
2 canned red peppers, cut into strips

Put the tomatoes, the chopped onions, garlic, parsley and ground walnuts in a bowl; mix them thoroughly and reserve.

Pour a tablespoon of olive oil over the bottom of a stewpan, lay out some of the tuna fillets and cover them with part of the reserved mixture and a seasoning of salt and pepper. Add further layers until all the fish and paste have been used, topping the sandwich with the strips of red pepper and another tablespoon of olive oil. Cover with a lid and cook slowly for about 20 minutes or until the fish is done. Serve with fried potatoes.

POLLO A LA CHILINDRON
CHICKEN IN CHILINDRON SAUCE

With its cheerful orange sauce, as spicy as it looks, this is one of the best dishes from Aragon.

A little pork fat
A little olive oil
1 chicken of about 4 lb (2 kg), cut up
1 lb (½ kg) tomatoes, blanched and peeled
1 onion, chopped
2 cloves garlic, crushed
4 or 5 canned red peppers, cut into strips
Salt and pepper

Heat a little pork fat and olive oil, mixed in equal parts, in a frying pan and brown the pieces of chicken. Transfer them to a stewpot, add the tomatoes, chopped onion, crushed garlic and strips of red pepper, season with salt and pepper and cook slowly for 1 hour or until the chicken is tender. The tomatoes and peppers should provide enough liquid, but if necessary add a little white wine or water during cooking.

CORDERO EN CHILINDRON
LAMB IN CHILINDRON SAUCE

Chilindrón sauce is as much a favourite for lamb as for chicken.

Olive oil
1 onion, cut up
3 cloves garlic, chopped
2 sprigs parsley
1 large tomato, blanched and peeled
2½ oz (75 g) minced belly of pork
2 lb (1 kg) lamb, best end of neck, cut up
6 canned red peppers, cut into strips
Salt and pepper

Heat a little olive oil in a frying pan and add the cut-up onion, one chopped clove of garlic and a sprig of parsley. Fry slowly for 5 minutes, then stir in the tomato and continue frying for another 10 minutes.

Heat a little more oil in a stewpot and add the minced belly of pork and the cut-up lamb. Brown the meat, then add the remaining chopped cloves of garlic, the tomato sauce and the strips of red pepper. Season with salt and pepper, cover with a lid and cook slowly for 1 hour or until the meat is tender. Sprinkle with chopped parsley before serving.

Ternasco asado
Roast lamb Aragonese style

A favourite way of roasting lamb in the mountains of Aragon.

3 lb (1½ kg) leg of lamb (or other roasting joint)
Salt
7 oz (200 g) pork fat
Juice of 2 lemons
1 glass dry white wine

Put the joint in a roasting tin, season with salt, smear with pork fat, then pour the lemon juice and white wine over it. Preheat the oven and roast at 375°F/190°C/Mark 5, for 20 minutes per lb (½ kg), basting at intervals.

Cochifrito

Navarra and the Spanish Pyrenees produce a particularly tender milk-fed lamb, known as *Tres Madres* ('Three Mothers'), and this is the traditional way of cooking it.

Olive oil or pork fat
2 lb (1 kg) milk-fed lamb, cut up
1 onion, cut up
1 clove garlic, chopped
1 teaspoon sweet paprika powder
White pepper, freshly ground
1 tablespoon chopped parsley
Juice of 1 lemon
Salt

Heat some olive oil or pork fat in a stewpot, brown the pieces of lamb and add the chopped onion and garlic, the paprika, white pepper, parsley and lemon juice, together with a little salt. Cook slowly for about 1 hour – milk-fed lamb will require less time than meat from an older animal.

Serve from the stewpot with fried potatoes.

Chuletas de cordero a la Navarra
Lamb chops Navarre style

Yet another way of cooking lamb from a region which excels in it.

A little pork fat
A little olive oil
2 lb (1 kg) small lamb chops
2 oz (50 g) cooked ham, cut up
1 onion, chopped
1 lb (½ kg) tomatoes, blanched, peeled and chopped
Pinch of sugar
Salt
4 slices *chorizo* from Pamplona

Mix equal parts of pork fat and olive oil in a frying pan, get it hot and brown the chops. Remove them and put them in a preheated oven dish. Using the same pan and fat, fry the chopped ham and onion, and when the onion begins to yellow pour off the fat and add the chopped tomatoes, the sugar and a little salt, leaving them to cook gently together until blended. Pour this sauce over the chops, decorate with the sliced *chorizo* and bake in a hot oven (375° F/190°/Mark 5) for 20 minutes. Serve piping hot with fried potatoes.

Carne almendrada
Pork with almonds

2 lb (1 kg) foreloin of pork
3½ oz (100 g) almonds, shelled and blanched
1 hard-boiled egg
Salt and pepper
2 tablespoons milk
Flour
A little pork fat
1 glass red wine
1 glass water

Cut the meat open lengthwise with a sharp knife, but without severing it at the bottom, so that it opens like a book.

Meanwhile toast the almonds for a few minutes in the oven, then grind them in a mortar with the hard-boiled egg, pepper and salt, and the milk. Score the meat deeply and press the paste into the cuts, then close the two halves and bind them with string, without pulling it too tight. Dredge it in flour, fry briefly in hot pork fat to brown it, then transfer to a baking dish and pour over it what remains of the fat from frying and the glasses of wine and water. Roast in a preheated oven (425° F/220° C/Mark 7) for 1 hour, basting at intervals.

The results are even better – and this applies to roasts of pork in general – if the meat is rubbed with salt and pepper and a little crushed garlic an hour or two before cooking.

The same recipe with almonds works very well with lamb.

Melocotones con vino tinto
Peaches in red wine

4 fresh peaches
2 oz (60 g) caster sugar
2 glasses red wine
1 vanilla pod

Put the peaches into a bowl with boiling water, leave them for a minute or two, then pour off the hot water and add cold. The peaches may now be peeled like tomatoes. Cut them in two, remove the stones, and again divide the halves.

Dissolve the sugar in the wine and grate the vanilla pod into it. Soak the cut-up peaches in the liquid for 2 or 3 hours before serving them.

Manjar de monjas
Nuns' delight

A traditional sweet made by the nuns.

3½ oz (100 g) caster sugar
3½ oz (100 g) rice flour
17 fl. oz (½ litre) milk
1 cinnamon stick
Pinch of cinnamon powder

Put the sugar and rice flour into a saucepan and add the milk gradually, stirring with a wooden spoon. Bring it just short of the boil, add the cinnamon stick and simmer until the mix thickens – 5 minutes or a little more will probably be sufficient.

Pour on to a large serving dish, so that the sweet may spread out thinly. Once it is cold, cut it into squares and sprinkle with powdered cinnamon before serving.

Catalonia

In gastronomy, as in other matters, Catalonia is one of the richest and most individual regions of Spain. Spanish books on its cooking keep returning to the magic figure of some hundred different regional specialities; be that as it may, the terrain is exceptionally varied, with the great mountain spurs of the Pyrenees descending to the coastal plain of the Mediterranean and the Ebro delta, so that livestock, game, freshwater and saltwater fish, vegetables and fruit abound.

Catalan energy and individualism are firmly rooted in history. Like other parts of Spain it was overrun by the Moors during the early stages of the invasion, but the Catalans soon turned to their neighbours over the Pyrenees, the Franks, for help in expelling them. After a first disastrous incursion into Spain, when Charlemagne's rearguard was ambushed at Roncesvalles in 778, he and his successors enabled the Catalans to drive the Muslims back beyond the River Ebro. But if, for a time, the inhabitants of the region voluntarily accepted Carolingian suzerainty in the shape of the so-called *Marca Hispánica* or Spanish Mark, they were by no means willing to exchange Moorish domination for Frankish; and by the time of his death in 897, the founder of the House of Barcelona, Wilfred the Hairy, had achieved *de facto* separation of the principality from the Empire. Under successive Counts of Barcelona, Catalonia soon rose to be one of the most powerful states of the Mediterranean. A decisive step forward was the union with Aragon; mercantile and territorial expansion in the Mediterranean proceeded apace; and by the beginning of the fourteenth century, having occupied Sicily, Catalan soldiers and sailors ventured as far afield as Constantinople and actually founded the Sicilian Duchy of Athens, which survived until 1387.

A strength of mediaeval Catalonia was that one of its greatest rulers, James the Conqueror (1213-76), made over the territories conquered from the Moors to working farmers, instead of handing over the large estates to the nobility, as happened in Castile. In this way he stimulated a healthy agricultural economy; Castile, on the other hand, was to suffer for centuries from a grant of the monopoly in the wool trade to the large landowners and consequent uneconomic development of natural resources. The fortunes of Catalonia declined after its union with Castile under the Catholic Monarchs in 1479, but the spirit of Catalan independence has never been extinguished and a nineteenth-century revival made Barcelona the commercial capital of Spain.

It was only to be expected that a state as rich and as inventive as mediaeval Catalonia was not backward in the culinary arts, which received further stimulus from the large-scale importation of spices from the East (it was, in fact, the spice trade which motivated Catalan maritime expansion in the eastern Mediterranean). The *Llibre de Coch* of 1477 (see page 4), whose author, according to firmly-established tradition, accompanied his master, Alfonso the Magnanimous, on his campaigns in Naples, was only the first of a series of treatises on cooking. It was succeeded by works such as the anonymous *La Cuynera catalan o sian reglas utils, facils, seguras y economicas per cuynar bé* ('Catalan Cooking, or Useful, Easy, Reliable and Economical Rules for Cooking Well') and *Avisos o sian reglas sensillas a un principiant cuyner o cuynera, adaptadas a la capacitat dels menos instruits* ('Instructions on Sensible Rules for a Learner Chef or Cook, Adjusted to the Capacities of the Less Knowledgeable'), written by Felip Cirera, probably a functionary of the episcopal palace at Vich, down to the *Magnific manual de cuina práctica catalana* ('Magnificent Manual of Practical Catalan Cooking') by Ignacio Doménech, doyen of Spanish chefs during the early decades of the present century, in the heroic mould of an Escoffier.

Spanish writers stress that each small locality in Catalonia has its individual way of preparing traditional dishes, for example singling out the Costa Brava for its seafood. The difficulty with the Costa Brava, as with other intensively developed holiday areas, is that there is now hardly a village without its quota of hotels laid out for foreign tourists, and in the seas of fish-and-chips and prawn cocktails authentic Catalan dishes have often sunk without trace. If you wish to sample regional cooking, go inland to Gerona or some small town such as Sta Coloma de Farnés, or better still start your adventures with the knife and fork in Barcelona.

In many ways Barcelona *is* Catalonia. It gave its name to the ruling dynasty; was the seat of Catalonian sea power and mercantile enterprise; the birthplace of the *Usatges*, the code of civil liberties which preceded *Magna Carta* by almost a century; and the mainspring of the nineteenth-century *Renaixença*, which gave new life to the Catalan language and literature. It was also in Barcelona that a new working class first became aware of its human rights and political influence. It is a city of strange contrasts, with its Gothic Quarter of narrow streets and old buildings bounded abruptly by wide avenues lined with plane trees and reminiscent of a dustier, sunnier Paris.

The heart of the old city is the Ramblas, a tree-lined avenue with a central promenade, where the stalls selling flowers, books and caged birds stand cheek by jowl with the open-air cafés. Like Madrid, Barcelona possesses many sophisticated restaurants, such as the elegant Reno or Via Veneto, but the most rewarding area for regional food is in the streets off the Ramblas or in the harbour area at their lower end – it was the boast of that noted Spanish epicure Luis Antonio de Vega that you could walk into almost any small restaurant in Barcelona with your eyes shut and not be disappointed.

Catalonia possesses five basic sauces, of which pride of place must go to *alioli*, corresponding to the Provençal *aïoli*, known since Roman times (see page 2 and recipe on page 101). The others are *picada*, containing almonds and toasted hazelnuts; *chanfaina* (page 108); *sofrito*, the Catalan version of *salsa española* (see page 52), used the length and breadth of Spain; and *romesco* (page 105), made from a local variety of small dried pepper.

As might be expected of a region with a long Mediterranean seaboard, the fish soups are legion; and two fish dishes deserve special mention. The origins of *bullabesa*, akin to the Provençal *bouillabaisse* have already been discussed (page 4) and it has been said that 'The *bullabesa* is like a woman. Some prefer it dark, others blonde, and yet others the colour of a redhead; it remains a woman, always essentially the same and at the same time different.' *Zarzuela*, which takes its name from a Spanish word meaning a variety show, is a truly magnificent dish, containing a variety of shellfish and firm white fish, cooked in a rich sauce containing onions, garlic and tomatoes.

Dried vegetables are often stewed with the delicate white *butifarra* sausage, made from minced pork, spices and a little of the blood, which are then filled into sausage skins, cooked and hung up to dry. Some of the best *butifarras*, which may also be eaten on their own, come from the old cathedral town of Vich, in the foothills of the Pyrenees. One of the best-known of such stews is *butifarra amb mongetes*, made with the local haricot beans.

Chicken and turkey are favourites with the Catalans, and there is no shortage of game like quail and partridge (see page 108). Another intriguing dish is rabbit cooked with snails.

Among the best of the sweets is *crema quemada a la catalana*, a baked custard topped by a thin layer of brittle caramel.

Catalonia produces a variety of excellent wines. Starting in the north, Perelada in the foothills of the Pyrenees makes a sparkling wine by the *cuves-closes* system, using large pressurized tanks. Some ten years ago it was the subject of a lawsuit in London, as a result of which the French champagne firms obtained judgment against the use of the name 'Spanish champagne'; it is nevertheless a pleasant enough and inexpensive sparkling wine of its type.

The vineyards of Alella, further south on the approaches of Barcelona, date from Roman times. Production is small, but the wines, both red and white, are soft and fruity. Perhaps the best is the white 'Marfil' ('Ivory') made by the old-established cooperative, which ages all its wine in oak for one or two years. Of its two whites, the *seco* (dry) goes better with food other than sweets, but the rather sweeter version is a rounder, fruitier wine.

Penedès, the other side of Barcelona, makes red and white table wines and also most of the best Spanish sparkling wine. The best of the still wines are from the Bodegas Torres, made scrupulously by the methods of Bordeaux. Its 'Sangre de Toro' – not to be confused with the wine of the same name from Toro – is inexpensive and full-bodied, while the 'Gran Coronas Reservas' are first-rate red wines, mature and velvety with a deep and satisfying bouquet. Its 'Viña Sol' is again an excellent dry white wine.

The sparkling wines from Penedès are produced by the champagne method, and the underground cellars of the largest firm, Codorniú, are said to be the most extensive in the world and have been designated a National Monument. Although these sparkling wines are not made from the same grapes as those from Rheims, they are elaborated with the greatest care and the quality is excellent. Much of the sweeter wine is exported to South America, and if your taste is for dry champagne ask for the '*bruto*'. If passing through Penedès, which is off the motorway south from Barcelona, make a point of visiting its wine museum, which is one of the best in the world, with exhibits illustrating not only the history of wine-making in Egypt, Greece and Rome, but in all the regions of Spain.

A feature of its exhibits are the long-spouted glass *porrones*, still used in small *tabernas* (and so popular with visitors as souvenirs), which gave rise to the *cri de coeur* from Alexandre Dumas:

> One of the most unexpected difficulties faced by the traveller is the way in which he is expected to drink in certain regions of Spain, particularly Navarra and Lower Aragon. It is rare to find

> glasses, and since drinking is a necessity, it is customary to put on the table a sort of bottle holding a litre or half-a-litre. Each member of the party must drink from it without touching the bottle with his lips. This is most uncomfortable for the unskilled stranger; and if he has the misfortune to touch it with his lips, his drinking companions pour the contents over his face and heap him with insults.

The coastal area around the pleasant resort of Sitges, south of Barcelona, is noted for its sweet dessert wines made from the white Sumoll and Malvasia grapes, which are allowed to wrinkle on the vines before being picked. Tarragona, further down the coast, capital of the Roman province of Tarraconensis covering the north-eastern part of the Peninsula, is rich in Roman remains, including massive surrounding walls, an aqueduct and the ruins of the forum. Its Gothic cathedral, built on a site earlier occupied by a temple to Jupiter and a Moorish mosque, is rich in sculpture and primitive paintings. It is now one of the main centres for the blending and shipping of wine in bulk – of the sort sold in off-licences as 'Spanish Burgundy' or 'Spanish Chablis'. The great *Bodegas de Exportación* line the dusty streets around the harbour, to which one of them is indeed connected by a pipeline capable of delivering 150,000 litres an hour to waiting tankers.

Among Tarragona's best-selling products are 'altar wine', supplied to the Vatican among other customers, and bottled *sangria*, made by adding commercial citrus essence to red wine. *Sangria* is a most refreshing drink on a hot day, but it is best made fresh by pouring a bottle of red wine into a large jug, adding ice cubes, sliced orange and lemon, a sprig of fresh mint, soda water or 'fizzy' lemonade, and a glass of Spanish brandy, and stirring well.

Tarragona also produces a variety of well-known vermouths under licence and from 1903 to 1940 was the refuge of the Carthusians from Grenoble after their expulsion from France. They established a distillery for making their famous Chartreuse, which is still in operation for supplying the Spanish and South American markets. The three monks who share the secret of the closely-guarded recipe and compound the herbs under lock and key, spend January to May in Tarragona and the rest of the year at the new distillery at Voiron. Visitors are welcome, and the tour ends with a tasting in the elegant *salón de degustación*, which houses a fascinating collection of fraudulent imitations.

Recipes

ALIOLI
GARLIC SAUCE

This classic Catalan sauce is served cold with grills, roast meat, fish and vegetables. A variety of other ingredients are sometimes incorporated in the basic recipe, often an egg yolk.

3 cloves garlic peeled
Salt
2 tablespoons chopped parsley
1 teacup (1½ dl) refined olive oil
Lemon juice

Crush the garlic in a mortar with a little salt and the parsley. Drip in the olive oil little by little, stirring all the while with a wooden spoon, add the lemon juice and continue stirring until it thickens like a mayonnaise.

SALSA VINAGRETA PARA PESCADOS COCIDOS
VINAIGRETTE SAUCE FOR FISH

2 anchovies, drained
2 tablespoons finely chopped onion
1 tablespoon chopped parsley
A little tarragon
Yolks of 3 hard-boiled eggs
7 fl. oz (2 dl) olive oil
2 tablespoons vinegar
Salt and pepper
2 dessertspoons capers

Pound the anchovies in a mortar, add the chopped onion, parsley and tarragon and blend into a smooth paste. Now incorporate the hard-boiled egg yolks and rub the mixture through a sieve and into a bowl. Drip in the olive oil little by little, stirring with a wooden spoon as if making a mayonnaise. Once the sauce begins to thicken, drip in the vinegar, continue stirring, season with pepper and salt and finally add the capers.

SOPA DE PESCADO
FISH SOUP

A soup with the taste of the sea, which may be made with any firm white fish.

1 lb (½ kg) firm white fish
Salt
Olive oil
2 onions, chopped
7 oz (200 g) tomatoes, blanched, peeled and chopped
1 teaspoon parsley, chopped
1 clove garlic, crushed
1 small packet saffron
2 oz (50 g) almonds, shelled
2 oz (50 g) French bread, thinly sliced

First cover the fish with cold salted water and simmer for about 10 minutes; then drain, reserving the stock. Put the fish on a plate, remove the skin and bones, then cut up the fish and reserve.

Heat a little olive oil in another saucepan, fry the onions until golden, drain off excess oil, then stir in the chopped tomatoes, parsley and garlic. Meanwhile pound the saffron and almonds in a mortar so as to make a paste. Add this and the fish stock to the contents of the saucepan, together with a little more water and salt if necessary, and simmer for ½ hour. Strain the liquid through a sieve, return it to the pan, add the pieces of fish, check the seasoning, and once the saucepan is on the boil again drop in the sliced bread. Remove from the fire without delay, cover with a lid, and leave for 5 minutes before serving.

SOPA DE MEJILLONES CATALANA
CATALAN MUSSEL SOUP

A variation on *moules marinières.*

2 lb (1 kg) mussels
A little olive oil
1 onion, chopped
3 tomatoes, blanched, peeled and cut up
3½ oz (100 g) toasted breadcrumbs
1 glass *aguardiente* (see page 147) or brandy
2 cloves garlic
Parsley
Pinch of cinnamon
Salt and pepper

Wash the mussels in changes of cold water and scrape the shells with a knife to clean them, then bring them to the boil in about 2 pints (12 dl) of salted water. Remove the mussels with a draining spoon and reserve the water in which they were cooked, straining it through muslin to get rid of grit.

Heat a little olive oil in a saucepan and fry the onion for about 10 minutes until it changes colour. Stir in the chopped tomatoes, cook gently until the mixture is smooth, then add the reserved stock, if necessary with enough extra water to provide for four servings. Bring to the boil, add the breadcrumbs and *aguardiente* and simmer for 5 minutes. Beat well with a wooden spoon to make sure that the breadcrumbs are smoothly incorporated. Meanwhile make a paste by grinding the garlic, parsley and cinnamon in a mortar with a little pepper and salt, and add this to the broth with the mussels. Leave to stand for 2 to 3 minutes before serving.

Sopa de albondiguillas catalana
Catalan soup with meat balls

4 oz (120 g) minced pork
2 oz (60 g) fresh belly of pork, minced
1 clove garlic, crushed
1 tablespoon chopped parsley
Pinch of cinnamon
Salt and pepper
1 egg
Flour
Olive oil
2 pints (12 dl) stock, made with a cube
2 oz (60 g) fresh breadcrumbs
Chervil
1 tablespoon tomato purée

Put into a bowl the minced pork and belly of pork, the garlic, parsley, a little cinnamon, salt and pepper, and the raw egg, and knead with the hands to make balls about the size of a hazelnut. Dredge them in flour, fry in hot olive oil and reserve.

Bring the stock to the boil in a saucepan, then stir in the breadcrumbs and beat to thicken the broth. Now add the meat balls, chervil, a little more parsley and the tomato purée and simmer gently for 15 minutes before serving.

Parrillada de pescado con salsa romesco
Mixed grilled fish with romesco sauce

This dish is at its best in Spain when the fish are grilled over a wood fire. In making it, you must obviously choose from the fish available at the time.

Fish

4 scampi
4 large prawns
8 mussels, well scraped and washed
8 clams, well scraped and washed
4 medium slices sea bass
4 red mullet
4 slices of hake
Olive oil
Salt

The fish are simply sprinkled with a little olive oil and grilled. The shellfish will open with the heat.

Romesco sauce

As explained (page 98), the sauce takes its name from the small red peppers used in making it.

3 dried Romesco peppers
10 toasted almonds
3 cloves garlic, crushed
3 medium-sized tomatoes, blanched, peeled, chopped and without pips
1 slice fried bread, crumbled
Pinch white pepper
4 fl. oz (125 ml) refined olive oil
4 fl. oz (125 ml) vinegar

Soak the peppers in tepid water for ½ hour, remove the seeds and drain, then grind them in a mortar with the almonds. Blend this paste with the crushed garlic, tomatoes, fried breadcrumbs and a little pepper, and transfer the mixture to a bowl. Now add the olive oil gradually, stirring with a wooden spoon as if making mayonnaise. Continue with the addition of the vinegar and a pinch of salt. Cover the bowl and leave it for 2 hours in the refrigerator, then check the seasoning and serve the sauce on the side with the *parrillada*.

Salsa romesco also goes well with other fish, vegetables and grilled meat.

Zarzuela de mariscos

You may ring the changes on this magnificent fish stew, provided that all the white fish is firm and does not disintegrate in cooking.

7 oz (200 g) angler fish, sliced
7 oz (200 g) rock bass or hake, sliced
8 clams
Olive oil
1 onion, chopped
7 oz (200 g) conger-eel, sliced
7 oz (200 g) inkfish (squid), cleaned and
 cut up (see page 24)
7 oz (200 g) prawns, in shell
4 scampi
1 clove garlic, crushed
A little tomato purée
2 glasses dry white wine
Salt and pepper
A little chopped parsley
1 small packet saffron, ground

First clean, wash and dry the white fish. Bring the clams to the boil in water, leave them until they open, then drain and reserve them.

Heat a little olive oil in a large pan, fry the chopped onion for 10 minutes, then add the sliced conger-eel, inkfish, angler fish, sea bass or hake, and the prawns and scampi, together with the crushed garlic, tomato purée and white wine. Season with salt, pepper and parsley, stir well together, then cook slowly for 20 minutes. 10 minutes before removing from the fire add the clams and ground saffron.

Langosta a la catalana
Lobster Catalan style

In Catalonia the dish is made with *langosta*, the spiny Mediterranean lobster or sea crayfish, which differs from the ordinary lobster – to which the recipe is equally applicable – in having no claws, but a couple of long antennae. There are a number of widely differing recipes for *langosta a la catalana*, some of them employing the blood of the live lobster and bitter chocolate. This version is more akin to lobster *à l'Américaine*, which does not, of course, hail from America, but was of Mediterranean or French origin.

If you are starting with a live lobster it must first be killed by plunging it into boiling water for a few minutes. The head should then be cut off and the lobster cut in two lengthwise. The only inedible parts are the bitter intestinal tract, a dark line running the length of the abdomen, and a small jelly-like sac in the head, which must be discarded. It is more likely that you will be buying a lobster already boiled by the fishmonger; and the procedure in both cases is now the same.

1 lobster of 2 lb (1 kg)
A little olive oil
A little pork fat
2 small onions, finely chopped
2 carrots, scraped and finely chopped
1 glass brandy
½ lb (225 g) tomatoes, blanched, peeled and chopped
Salt and pepper
Nutmeg

Remove the lobster meat from the two half-shells, keeping them for later use. If you are using an ordinary lobster rather than *langosta*, crack the claws, remove the meat and add it to the rest. Now heat a little mixed olive oil and pork fat in a pan and fry the chopped onions and carrots for 10 minutes. Add the lobster meat, stir briefly, then pour in the brandy and allow to reduce a little. Add the tomatoes and spices, cook gently for another 15 minutes, then fill back the meat into the half-shells. Rub what remains in the pan through a sieve or put it into a blender so as to make a smooth sauce. Pour this over the half-shells, place them under the grill for a minute or two and serve piping hot.

Perdiz a la catalana
Partridge Catalan style

Per person:

1 partridge
A little olive oil
1 dessertspoon flour
¾ pint (450 ml) meat broth
Salt and pepper
Bouquet garni of bay leaf, thyme and origanum
2 cloves garlic, chopped
2 slices lemon

Brown the partridge in hot olive oil and put it into a saucepan. Using the same oil and pan, stir in the flour and when it has soaked up the oil, add the meat broth, a little pepper and salt, the *bouquet garni* and garlic. Stir together, then pour the liquid over the partridge and cook very slowly for about an hour or until the bird is tender. Serve on a dish decorated with the slices of lemon.

Pollo en chanfaina
Chicken in chanfaina sauce

Method of cooking chicken in a piquant sauce, somewhat reminiscent of the *chilindrón* from neighbouring Aragon.

Olive oil
3 courgettes, washed and cup up
2 red or green peppers, deseeded and cut up
2 onions, chopped
1 lb 2 oz (500 g) tomatoes, blanched, peeled and cut up
2 cloves garlic, crushed
1 small glass dry white wine or sherry
1 bay leaf
Thyme
Salt
Black pepper
1 chicken of 3 lb (1½ kg), cut up
Flour
Squares of fried bread

Heat some olive oil in a pan and fry together the cut-up courgettes, peppers and onions for some 10 minutes. Drain off the excess oil, add the chopped tomatoes and garlic and cook gently for another 10 minutes until the tomatoes are soft. Now stir in the wine, herbs and spices, remove from the fire and transfer to a stewpot, while you prepare the chicken.

Reheat the oil in the same frying pan, if necessary adding a little more, dredge the pieces of chicken in flour, brown them and then transfer them with a draining spoon to the stewpot. Cook slowly on top of the stove for 1½ hours or until the chicken is tender, then serve surrounded by squares of fried bread and fried potatoes.

GARBANZOS A LA CATALANA
CHICK-PEAS CATALAN STYLE

A main dish containing the delicious *butifarra* sausage, so typical of the region.

1 lb 5 oz (600 g) chick-peas
Salt
2 oz (60 g) pork fat
1 onion, finely chopped
4 tomatoes, blanched, peeled and cut up
2 oz (50 g) pine kernels
5 oz (150 g) *butifarra* (see page 98)
Salt and pepper
4 eggs, hard-boiled and shelled

Soak the chick-peas overnight in lukewarm water, rinsing and draining them next day.

Bring sufficient salted water to the boil in a stewpot, add the chick-peas and cook slowly for 1½ hours. Now strain off the liquid into another pan through a colander, reserving the chick-peas. Meanwhile heat the pork fat in a pan, fry the chopped onion for about 15 minutes until golden, then add the tomatoes and cook slowly for another 10 minutes. Stir in the pine kernels and *butifarra* with a wooden spoon, then transfer the mixture to a stewpot and add the cooked chick-peas. Stir briefly, then pour in the reserved vegetable stock, season with salt and pepper, and simmer for another hour or hour-and-a-half until the chick-peas are tender. Sprinkle with grated hard-boiled egg before serving.

Costillas con alioli
Ribs of pork with alioli sauce

16 ribs of pork on the bone
Salt
Alioli sauce (see page 101)

Separate the ribs with a knife, place them between greaseproof paper and flatten them with the side of a meat cleaver. Your butcher can do this for you. They are best cooked on a charcoal grill, sprinkled with a little salt. Serve with alioli sauce.

Orelletas de Tarragona
Sweet pancakes from Tarragona

½ oz (15 g) dried yeast
1 lb 5 oz (500 g) flour, sieved
3½ oz (100 g) caster sugar
3 eggs
1 liqueur glass anisette or Pernod
Peel of 1 lemon, grated
Olive oil
Icing sugar

Reconstitute the dried yeast according to the instructions on the container, then put all the ingredients except the olive oil and icing sugar into a bowl and knead into a dough. If necessary, add a little milk before rolling it out on a pastry board or marble slab. Weigh out portions of about 1 oz (30 g), roll them out into thin pancakes and fry in hot olive oil until golden. Serve them either hot or cold, powdered with icing sugar.

Dulces de Tarragona
A sweet from Tarragona

1 lb 5 oz (500 g) flour, sieved
1 lb 5 oz (500 g) almonds, minced
3 eggs
Peel of 1 lemon, grated
11 oz (300 g) caster sugar

Put all the ingredients into a bowl, mix and knead them into a smooth dough, then roll it out on a pastry board or marble slab and cut it into pieces like shortbread fingers. Now grease an oven sheet and bake them at moderate heat (350° F/180° C/Mark 4) for about 20 minutes to ½ hour until golden.

Crema quemada a la catalana
Baked custard with brittle caramel

6 yolks of egg
1 oz (25 g) cornflour
11 oz (320 g) icing sugar
17 fl. oz (½ litre) milk
1 cinnamon stick
Peel of 1 lemon

Beat the egg yolks in a bowl with the cornflour and 6 oz (170 g) of the icing sugar. Simmer the milk with the cinnamon stick and lemon peel, then add the egg mixture and cook slowly, stirring continuously to avoid lumps, until the custard thickens. Now remove the cinnamon and lemon peel, pour the custard into a serving dish and leave to cool. Finally, sprinkle the surface with the rest of the icing sugar and press lightly on it with a palette knife, heated in a gas flame, so as to form a brittle layer of caramel on the top.

The Balearics

Standing in the great hall of Palma airport, thronged with tourists in their thousands waiting to take off for Hamburg or Manchester in their jumbo jets, it is difficult to realize that until the tourist boom of the early 1950s, Majorca and the smaller islands of Minorca, Ibiza and Formentera were deserted and impoverished, a haven for romantics, such as George Sand and Chopin – little as they enjoyed their visit to Majorca during the winter of 1838-9.

Today, when every inch of beach seems to be flanked by hotels and high-rise apartments, there are still long stretches of coast too rocky for development; and in the mountainous interior the foreign invasion has actually resulted in depopulation, as the younger people migrate to Palma to work in the shops and hotels. All too frequently the solid stone houses of their forebears stand roofless; the olives and figs go unpicked; and the only noise to break into the silence of the surrounding mountains is the will-o'-the-wisp jingle of a goat-bell.

The islanders are of very mixed origin. Majorca in particular was a regular port of call for the Greeks and Phoenicians in their early trading expeditions to the mainland of the Peninsula, and they were followed by the Carthaginians and Romans. The Jews arrived in strength after their expulsion from Rome and the Holy Land and were for long the backbone of the professional and commercial classes, as are their Christianized descendants today. One of the greatest formative influences was the occupation of the Balearics by the Córdoban caliphate in AD 902. The Moors remained in firm possession for some centuries longer than on the mainland – even now many Majorcans are of Moorish appearance – and it was not until 1229 that James the Conqueror arrived off the western tip of Majorca with a large fleet and after stubborn fighting around Palma claimed the islands for the Crown of Aragon.

When James died in 1276 he left his kingdom divided between his two sons, Majorca going to the younger, James II. Thereafter, the attempts of the kings of Aragon to impose their suzerainty and the determination of the Majorcan branch of the dynasty to remain independent, resulted in long drawn-out hostilities, until Pedro the Ceremonious finally incorporated the islands in the Crown of Aragon by his defeat of the last King of Majorca, Pedro III, in 1349. Cultural and linguistic ties with Catalonia and the bordering provinces of France, which were also for long dominated by the House of Barcelona, remained close; and the Mallorquín spoken in the islands today is very similar to Catalan and the dialect of the Languedoc.

It is of interest that the neighbouring island of Minorca was ruled for most of the eighteenth century by the British, after a squadron under Sir John Leake took its capital, Port Mahón, in 1708 during the War of the Spanish Succession. It reverted to Spain in 1782, when Charles III took advantage of Britain's involvement in the American War of Independence to regain it.

Ties with Catalonia are reflected in the native cooking, which is basically peasant in character and dependent on local ingredients. Only in the last decades, when the summertime population has swollen by some 50 per cent thanks to the influx of tourists, has it been found necessary to import food and wine in large amounts from the mainland; cooking in the modern hotels is, of course, of the 'international' variety. Restaurants in Palma change hands so quickly and so obviously cater for visitors that it is difficult to recommend places serving authentic Majorcan dishes; but the seafood, fresh from its magnificent harbour, is splendid in whatever guise. There seems little reason to doubt that the mayonnaise served with the splendid lobsters takes its name from Port Mahón (see page 2), although other and less convincing derivations have been put forward.

Meat is much less varied than fish; the best is pork in its different forms. As in Catalonia and the Extremadura, the *matanza* or 'killing of the pig' is an annual festival in country regions and owed its origin to the need for laying in supplies of preserved meat at the onset of winter. The *embutidos*, made by salting, spicing and smoking the various cuts and innards of the animal, include *chorizo* (page 116) and the delicate white *butifarra* (page 98) – indeed in Majorca the rich and self-important are scathingly known as *butifarrones* in likeness to a swelling sausage. Perhaps most typical of the Balearics is the soft orange *sobrasada*, made by stirring finely minced pork with salt, sweet paprika powder and a little cayenne pepper, then filling the mixture into the tripes and hanging up the sausages to dry without cooking. It may be spread on bread, or when stirred into a stew forms a ready-made and piquant sauce.

The basis of many native dishes is the excellent vegetables. Good examples are the famous *sopa mallorquina* (page 118) and *tumbet* (page 119), a variation on *ratatouille*, containing potatoes, onions, tomatoes and courgettes.

Until the latter part of the eighteenth century olive trees were even more prolific than almonds, and the olive oil is still of the best. Large-scale planting of almonds began after the mid-eighteenth century, and in the early spring Majorca is a sea of white blossom. The harvest starts towards the end of August. With the drift of younger people to Palma, the whole remaining population of the villages, including old women and children, is pressed into service. The fruit is first shaken down on to large canvas sheets, the tough green skin is then cut off and the nuts are left to dry in the sun and then despatched in sacks for cracking, roasting or milling. The female kernels, which occur in pairs, are usually ground for confectionery, while the larger male nuts are roasted or salted.

The Balearics grow beautiful figs and oranges, and an exotic is the prickly pear, which grows wild in the fields and by the roadside. Its sweetish flavour somewhat resembles that of an ordinary pear – but approach the glowing fruit with respect. If possible, use a pair of old gloves in picking and handling it. In any case, before removing the skin the tufts of fine spines should be scraped off with a knife – otherwise they will most certainly and painfully penetrate your fingers.

The pomegranate is another fruit which requires careful preparation. After stripping off the skin and digging out the seeds in their gelatinous envelopes, carefully remove the bitter-tasting white connective membrane. What remains may be eaten fresh with a little sugar and sherry, but is always somewhat astringent and, of course, very gritty because of the large size of the pips. Perhaps the best way of dealing with pomegranates is to stew the seeds with sugar and to strain off the pink juice, which goes excellently with roast lamb.

The islands, especially Minorca, produce a good semi-hard cheese with a full flavour, the *queso de Mahón*, made from cow's milk, not in rounds, but in large rectangular cakes with rounded corners.

Majorcan bread is baked in flat rounds. It looks attractive, but is heavy in texture, and indeed the islanders prefer to eat it when it is a few days old. It is also sold in dried shavings for adding to soups. In complete contrast are the *ensaimadas*, eaten with coffee or chocolate for breakfast, and perhaps the only genuinely Majorcan speciality to be served in the holiday hotels. Light, fluffy, a little sweet and halfway between a bun and a pastry, it resembles a Moorish turban in shape. It seems that *ensaimadas* cannot be properly made except in the islands, and large consignments are regularly shipped to Barcelona and the mainland.

Coca mallorquina (page 120), on the other hand, which resembles an Italian *pizza*, is made from a substantial pasta, in which are embedded strips of onion, pepper and tomato, sometimes with the addition of anchovies or tuna. It was traditionally, and is still, cooked by the peasants in their outdoor ovens of stone or brick. The oven is fired with wood or almond shells and allowed to heat until the black deposit of carbon is burnt off the domed roof. The fire is then raked out, the trays of *coca* are slid in, the arched aparture at the front is stopped up and the *coca* baked for an hour or two until ready. Portions of *coca* may be bought in any *confitería* (confectioner's shop) to take away for a picnic; they also sell a great variety of cakes and sweetmeats, among the *turrones* (see page 34) made from ground almonds.

The outdoor ovens used for cooking bread or *coca* are distinct from those to be found in every traditional Majorcan kitchen. These were fired by charcoal, shovelled into long channels in the brickwork and kept aglow with a fan. Very beautiful they were with their decorative tiled fronts, but they have now almost entirely been replaced by butane gas cookers, since charcoal burning, once an important industry, has fallen into almost total abeyance.

A great deal of the wine sold in hotels and restaurants is shipped from the mainland, and there is no difficulty in obtaining the well-known brands of sherry and Rioja. It is, of course, much more interesting to experiment with what the islands themselves produce. The main wine-growing areas in Majorca are in the central plain, around Santa María, Inca and Binisalem to the west, which produce the best of the red wine, and Felanitx to the east. A pleasant and leisurely way of reaching these places is by the narrow gauge railway which winds through the almond groves and the windmills used for pumping water for irrigation. Originally built by an English company and equipped with locomotives and rolling stock from Manchester and Birmingham, it is now operated with small diesels.

Much of the *vino corriente* is made in cooperatives, of which the largest is at Felanitx. These local wines are usually 'earthy' and heavy and may be sampled in any small taberna or bar. If you ask for Majorcan wine in a more expensive restaurant, you will almost certainly be given one of those made by José L. Ferrer at his bodegas in Binisalém. These are the best Majorca has to offer and are available as 'Binisalém Auténtico', 'Tinto Franja Roja' and *reservas* of different vintages, all red. Oddly enough, the modestly-priced 'Auténtico' available at the time of writing often carries an earlier date than the *reserva*, and there does not seem to be a great deal to choose between the three wines currently on sale, all of which share the somewhat dry, peppery taste of the better growths from around Valencia or Jumilla – though we are informed by Majorcan friends that the old *reservas* are very fine. These wines have a tendency to develop turbidity in the bottle, which does not in our experience affect the flavour – the only response you are likely to obtain from a Majorcan wine waiter is an affirmation that he prefers Binisalem to Rioja. They are not made in sufficient quantity to export in any considerable amount.

The thirst of the summer visitors is such that the islands are net importers of wine. This was not always the case, since large amounts of Majorcan wine went to France during the outbreak of phylloxera, but the native vineyards never recovered their former extent after Majorca was itself affected by the disease in 1891. That pioneer of Victorian wine writers, Cyrus Redding, spoke approvingly of 'a very good red wine, called Aleyor'; and both San Luis and Alayor in Minorca still make wines of local repute.

Recipes

SALSA MAHONESA
MAYONNAISE

According to a well-established historical tradition mayonnaise originated in Port Mahón (see page 2) and, in various forms, is a great favourite in the Balearic Islands. The basic recipe follows:

2 egg yolks
1 teaspoon mustard powder
1 teaspoon salt
1 clove garlic, crushed
Olive oil (roughly ½ pint or 3 dl)
Juice of 1 lemon, or equivalent amount of refined vinegar

Method with a blender: The simplest method of making mayonnaise without danger of its thickening or curdling is to use a blender. Put the egg yolks, mustard, salt and garlic into the blender and mix at medium speed. Trickle in the olive oil, mixing at the same speed, until the mayonnaise has thickened. Add the lemon juice or 1 tablespoon of wine vinegar and blend at the highest speed for a few seconds. It may be kept in the refrigerator in a screwtop jar and used when required.

Method without a blender: Break the egg yolks into a large bowl and beat with the crushed garlic, salt and mustard powder. Add the olive oil little by little, beating with a wooden spoon until the mayonnaise thickens. If it shows signs of curdling, beat in another egg yolk. Once the mayonnaise has thickened, trickle in the lemon juice or vinegar and stir well.

The garlic is not to everyone's taste and may be omitted.

Salsa mahonesa verde
Green mayonnaise

This goes well with fish.

1 oz (30 g) spinach
1 oz (30 g) watercress
1 oz (30 g) tarragon
1 oz (30 g) chervil
1 oz (30 g) parsley
Salt
Mayonnaise (see above)

Boil all the vegetables together for 8 minutes with a little salt. Drain and rub through a sieve, or alternatively put the cooked vegetables into a blender, so as to obtain a smooth purée. When cold, this is added to the mayonnaise in the required amount and stirred in with a wooden spoon.

Salsa tartara
Tartare sauce

Often served in the Balearics, as elsewhere, with fish or cold chicken.

2 cups mayonnaise (see above)
1 egg, hard-boiled and chopped
12 capers
3 or 4 gherkins, finely chopped
Chopped chives or parsley

Stir the ingredients into the mayonnaise, adding a little chopped chives or parsley at the last moment.

Sopa mallorquina
Majorcan soup

Olive oil
2 cloves garlic, chopped
2 onions, chopped
1 lb (½ kg) cabbage or spring vegetables, washed and chopped
1 teaspoon sweet paprika
Salt
3½ oz (100 g) stale bread
A little chopped parsley

Grocers in Majorca sell a special hard bread, almost a rusk and thinly sliced, for this soup. Perhaps the best equivalent abroad is shavings of bread from a stale French loaf or melba toast.

Heat some olive oil in a saucepan and fry the garlic very briefly, taking care that it does not blacken, then remove with a draining spoon and reserve. Now fry the chopped onions for about 5 minutes until they change colour, then stir in the vegetables and season with paprika and salt. Add 2½ pints (1½ litres) of water or stock, together with the reserved garlic, and simmer for about ½ hour. Add the bread and cook for another 5 minutes before sprinkling in the parsley, checking the seasoning and serving.

Caldereta de datiles de mar

This soup is made in Majorca and in the Levante with the small brown *dátiles de mar* ('sea dates'); elsewhere mussels may be used.

2 lb (1 kg) *dátiles* or mussels
2 oz (50 g) pork fat
A little olive oil
1 sprig parsley
2 cloves garlic, crushed
9 fl. oz (¼ litre) fish stock or water
1 glass dry white wine
Salt and pepper
1 teaspoon sweet paprika powder

If using *dátiles*, wash them thoroughly; mussels must be scraped with a knife. Now reserve the shellfish on a plate. Heat the mixed pork fat and olive oil in a stewpan and then add the sprig of parsley, crushed garlic, *dátiles*, fish stock and white wine, together with a little salt and pepper and the teaspoon of paprika powder. Cover with the lid, cook gently until the *dátiles* open, and serve from the stewpan. In Spain the soup is made in a deep earthenware *cazuela*.

More sophisticated cooking. Chickens grilling outside Los Caracoles restaurant in the old city of Barcelona

Facing page, top left Son Torrella de Santa María, a baronial house in Majorca

Facing page, top right A Majorcan windmill, used for irrigating the land

Facing page, bottom left An outdoor Majorcan oven for making bread or *coca*, a delicacy resembling the Italian *pizza*

Facing page, bottom right *Cocas*, with the spade-shaped instrument used for removing them from the hot oven

Above Majorca is famous for its seafood. Fishing boats in the harbour at Palma, with the Cathedral in the background

Top Baronial houses at Santillana del Mar near Santander. One of the most famous of the *Paradores* is located in a similar house opposite

Left The menu of the atmospheric Bodega del Riojano in Santander was designed by Picasso

Habas al estilo de Mahon
Broad beans Minorcan style

This is an example of how the soft *sobrasada* sausage (see page 113), which dissolves during cooking, is used to add flavour to a vegetable dish.

2 lb (1 kg) shelled fresh or frozen broad beans
Salt and pepper
1 lb (½ kg) potatoes, peeled and cut up
1 onion, chopped fine
1 large tomato, blanched and peeled
1 courgette, peeled and sliced
7 oz (200 g) *sobrasada*
2 tablespoons olive oil

Cover the beans with cold water, add a little salt and pepper, then bring to the boil and cook for 15 to 20 minutes until tender. Add the other ingredients and simmer for another ½ hour. Check the seasoning before serving.

Tumbet
Majorcan egg and vegetable pie

Olive oil
8 oz (225 g) potatoes, peeled and sliced
8 oz (225 g) red peppers, deseeded and cut up
8 oz (225 g) onions, cut into rings
8 oz (225 g) courgettes, sliced
1 pint (6 dl) *salsa española* (see page 52)
4 eggs, beaten

Fry separately in hot olive oil the rounds of potato, the cut-up peppers, onion rings and sliced courgettes. Drain and reserve on separate plates. Grease a large fireproof dish and lay a first layer of the cooked vegetables on the bottom, cover with *salsa española* and beaten egg, and continue with alternate layers of vegetables, *salsa española* and beaten egg until all the ingredients are used up.

Cook in a moderate oven (325° F/170° C/Mark 3) for 1 hour or until crisp and golden.

Huevos a la mallorquina
Eggs Majorcan style

Eggs cooked with vegetables in this very individual way make a good supper dish.

½ lb (225 g) carrots, scraped and sliced
3 leeks, washed and cut up
17 fl. oz (½ litre) stock, made with a cube if stock unavailable
1 fl. oz (30 ml) milk
1 oz (30 g) butter
Salt and pepper
7 oz (200 g) *sobrasada* (see page 113) in 8 slices
8 eggs

Cook the vegetables in the stock for about 20 minutes, then drain them and rub through a sieve or put them in a blender. Add the milk and butter (reserving a little for the final stages), season with salt and pepper and make a purée, beating it as you would mashed potatoes.

Now line the bottom of an oven dish with the slices of *sobrasada*. Fry the eggs and lay them on top. Dot them with butter, then pour the vegetable purée over them and bake in a moderate oven (350° F/180° C/Mark 4) until browned.

Coca mallorquina

As described on page 115, this is an open tart resembling an Italian *pizza*.

Pastry
1 oz (25 g) dried yeast
A little milk
2 oz (50 g) pork fat
3½ oz (100 g) olive oil
1 lb 5 oz (500 g) flour, sieved

Dissolve the dried yeast in a little lukewarm milk in a bowl. Leave it for 5 minutes, add the pork fat and olive oil and then the flour, little by little, kneading the dough with your fingers until it no longer sticks to the side of the bowl. Shape the mass into a ball, return it to the bowl and leave it covered for 1 hour.

Topping

3 red or green peppers, deseeded and cut into strips
3 spring onions or 1 large onion, chopped
3 medium-sized tomatoes, blanched, peeled and sliced
1 clove garlic
A little parsley, chopped
Salt

Grease a rectangular baking tray and roll out the pasta, so that it forms a sheet about ⅓–½ inch (1 cm) thick. On this, spread out all the vegetables, finally crushing the garlic on to them, sprinkling on the parsley and seasoning with salt. Canned sardines or tuna, cut into pieces of suitable size, and also cooked spinach are often added to the layer of vegetables to give additional flavour. Finally, bake the *coca* in a preheated oven (350° F/180° C/Mark 4) for 20 to 30 minutes. It may be eaten either hot or cold and is a good stand-by for a picnic.

VISTA DE LA LONJA EN PALMA.

Tortilla de sardinas frescas
Sardine omelette

Made with fresh sardines, this has a flavour and fragrance altogether different from omelettes made with the tinned fish.

8 fresh sardines
Juice of 1 lemon
Olive oil
Salt
1 bay leaf
Freshly ground white pepper
1 teaspoon sweet paprika powder
1 onion, chopped fine
8 eggs

Clean and wash the sardines, removing the heads and backbones, then leave them open on a glass dish to marinate for ½ hour with the above ingredients, except for the onion and the eggs.

Now heat a little olive oil in a pan, fry the chopped onion for about 15 minutes, then add the sardines. Stir with the cooked onion and fry for another 10 minutes.

Meanwhile separate the yolks from the whites of the eggs. Whisk the whites until stiff, then stir in the yolks and beat for a little longer. Take a clean frying pan, add a little olive oil and get it really hot, then pour in the egg mixture, add the fish and shake vigorously. After a minute or two invert the omelette on to a plate, then, without adding more oil, slide it back into the pan to cook the other side. Serve golden-brown and with all speed.

Langosta a la mallorquina
Lobster Majorcan style

A Majorcan version of lobster mayonnaise, served hot.

6 tablespoons olive oil
3 tablespoons vinegar
Pepper
2 large lobsters, boiled (see pages 106-07)
Mayonnaise (see page 116)
1 lettuce
2 sticks celery

Make a sauce by mixing the olive oil, vinegar and pepper in a cup and beating until thick. Cut the lobsters lengthwise, sprinkle them with the sauce and put them under the grill (in Majorca they are often grilled in the open air over charcoal). Paint them with more of the dressing during cooking, leave them until browned, then pour on a little mayonnaise.

Serve with a salad of lettuce and chopped celery.

Calamares a la mallorquina
Stuffed inkfish Majorcan style

An entirely individual method of cooking inkfish, in which they are stuffed with pine kernels, sultanas and other ingredients.

4 inkfish (squid) of the same medium size
1 onion, finely chopped
3½ oz (100 g) seedless sultanas
2 oz (50 g) pine kernels
1 tablespoon fresh breadcrumbs
2 eggs, lightly beaten
Salt and pepper
A little olive oil
1 glass dry white wine

Wash and clean the inkfish (see page 24). Remove, chop and reserve the tentacles. Blanch the bodies of the inkfish by pouring boiling water onto them, leaving them for a few minutes and draining.

Now put the chopped tentacles into a bowl with the chopped onion, sultanas, pine kernels, breadcrumbs, beaten egg and a little salt and freshly-ground pepper, and stir well together. Fill this mixture into the cavities of the inkfish and sew them up with strong thread, so that the filling does not spill out during cooking.

Heat a little olive oil in a pan and fry the inkfish gently for ten minutes, shaking so that they do not stick. Now add the glass of white wine and leave over a low heat until the liquid has evaporated.

PERDICES DE CAPELLAN
CHAPLAIN'S 'PARTRIDGE'

Though not in fact made with partridge, this monastic fare is by no means lean.

Per person:
1 escalope of veal (2 oz, 60 g)
1 thin slice cooked ham
1 slice *sobrasada* (see page 113)
Flour
A little pork fat
1 red pepper, deseeded and cut up fine
2 cloves garlic, chopped
1 teaspoon mixed herbs
1 glass dry white wine
Freshly-ground pepper
Salt
Chopped parsley

The escalopes should be flattened and elongated in shape, and the ham of the same size and shape. Put the escalopes on a table, lay the slices of ham and *sobrasada* on top, then roll them up in the manner of a beef olive, secure them with thread and dredge in flour.

Now heat the pork fat in a frying pan, fry the rolled-up veal until golden, then transfer to a stewpan with a draining spoon. Using the same pan and oil, fry the chopped pepper for 5 minutes, then stir in the garlic, mixed herbs, white wine and a little freshly-ground pepper and salt, and cook gently for another 5 minutes. Pour this sauce on top of the veal in the stewpan and cook slowly for ½ hour. Remove the threads, sprinkle with parsley and serve with fried potatoes.

REVOLTILLO DE SOBRASADA

Revoltillo is often translated as 'scrambled eggs', but the Spanish method of stirring eggs in a smoking hot pan with tomatoes, chopped ham or other ingredients, is not the same as scrambling them, nor are the results at all like an omelette. This very savoury Balearic version employs the peppery *sobrasada* sausage.

2 tablespoons pork fat
7 oz (200 g) *sobrasada*, sliced and skinned
4 eggs

Heat the pork fat in a pan, add the slices of *sobrasada*, allow them to get hot without dissolving or blackening, then pour in the lightly beaten eggs and stir vigorously until cooked. The sausage is so highly seasoned that salt and pepper are not necessary. Serve with all speed.

Greixera mallorquina
Egg, cheese and bacon pie

This very traditional Majorcan dish takes its name from the shallow earthenware dish used for cooking it.

1 clove garlic
1 lb (500 g) grated cheese, e.g. Cheddar
4 eggs
1 tablespoon breadcrumbs
1 tablespoon flour
3½ oz (100 g) green bacon, finely chopped
A little pork fat

Crush the garlic into a large bowl and mix with the grated cheese. Add the eggs one by one, stirring well with a wooden spoon, then add the breadcrumbs, flour and the finely chopped green bacon and knead together. Now grease an oven dish, round if possible, with pork fat, smooth the mixture into it and bake in a medium oven (350° F/180° C/Mark 4) until golden-brown. Remove and leave for a few minutes to cool a little, otherwise the *greixera* will crumble when you cut it.

Lomo a la mallorquina
Loin of pork Majorcan style

A sandwich of pork and *sobrasada* sausage. Escalopes of veal may be cooked in exactly the same way by sandwiching them with ham.

8 small fillets of loin pork
Salt
4 slices *sobrasada*
1 egg, beaten
Breadcrumbs
Olive oil or pork fat for frying

First flatten the fillets by putting them between greaseproof paper and thumping them with the side of a meat-cleaver – or get the butcher to do this for you. Season with salt, then make the sandwiches with the *sobrasada* in the middle, secure them with broken-off cocktail sticks and dredge in beaten egg and breadcrumbs.

Heat the pork fat or olive oil in a pan and fry the meat, turning it from time to time until golden. Serve with fried potatoes.

Pastelitos mallorquines
Majorcan cup cakes

3 eggs
3½ oz (100 g) caster sugar
2 oz (50 g) rice flour, sieved
Peel of 1 lemon, grated
A little butter

Separate the whites from the yolks of the eggs and beat the whites stiff. Fold in the yolks, sugar, rice flour and grated lemon peel and stir well with a palette knife or wooden spoon.

Preheat the oven to 425° F/220° C/Mark 7, then turn it down to 375° F/190°/Mark 5. Meanwhile grease some small cake moulds with a little butter, pour the mixture into them and bake for 10 to 15 minutes or until golden-brown.

VISTA DEL CASTILLO DE BELLVER EN PALMA.

The Basque Provinces

It is generally accepted in Spain that the best and most varied cooking is to be found in the Basque provinces, flanking the Bay of Biscay. Spanish writers often refer to Bilbao as the country's gastronomic capital. As long ago as 1549, Pedro de Medina wrote in his *Libro de grandezas y cosas memorables de España* that 'Bilbao is a noble city of much quality, because three things are to be found there: pleasant situation, *abundance* of food and the good conduct of its people and merchants'. Both Bilbao and San Sebastián have long been renowned for their dining societies, where food is prepared by both men and women *socios* (or members). Gastronomes such as the Marqués de los Andes and Luis Antonio de la Vega are quick to point out that these gatherings are notable not only for the abundance of the fare, but for its sophistication. Good cooking stems from the quality of the materials; and the Basque country is blessed with dairy produce, vegetables and fruit from its green meadows and mountain pastures, and splendid fish from the cold waters of the Bay of Biscay.

The Basques themselves are as much of an historical enigma as their strange language. The most generally accepted theory is that they are the last survivors of the original Celtiberian inhabitants of the Peninsula. The most recent suggestion comes from no less a source than the pages of *Pravda*. A Soviet historian and philologist, Alexander Kiknadze, claims to have catalogued some 360 Basque words, similar or identical to those used in the Caucasus or present-day Georgia. Among them is the very name for the Peninsula itself, identical with that of Georgia (*Iveria*). As further evidence he cites an ancient tablet excavated in Bilbao, bearing an inscription only recently deciphered by Georgian scholars. This purports to describe a mass immigration from the east after a natural cataclysm in prehistoric times.

Be this as it may – and the idea has been considered worthy of investigation by the Society for the Defence of the Basque Language – the Basques have always displayed a lively independence. The region has not contributed to the mainstream of Spanish history. From the Romans and Moors to Napoleon's conquering armies, no foreign invader has established a lasting foothold. In Spain's internal struggles the Basques have always favoured the side that promised local autonomy, and thus supported the pretender Don Carlos during the Carlist Wars of the nineteenth century and the Republicans during the Civil War; their desire to rule themselves remains unabated today. The Basque country nevertheless makes a most important contribution to the Spanish economy; it is the headquarters of the country's steel-making and shipbuilding industries and of many of the important banks.

Given excellent materials and the wherewithal to indulge a taste for good cooking, which the Basques share with the Gascons across the border – both names come from the Latin source, *Vascones* – it is hardly surprising that they should be pre-eminent.

No one has written more poetically of the mystique of the sea than Pío Baroja in stories such as *The Restlessness of Shanti Andía*; and the Basques are hardy fishermen and sailors. Having braved their own stormy waters, they often turned to exploration and sometimes to piracy; it was a Basque, Juan Sebastián Elcano, who first circumnavigated the globe. The fishermen are themselves no mean cooks or trenchermen; at the beginning of the anchovy season in the spring, it was formerly the custom of the crews from Santoña to seal their compact with the owners of the boats, not in writing, but by sitting at table with them and sharing a copious meal. The famous *marmite*, made by stewing tuna with onion, garlic and potatoes, was often prepared on board the fishing craft and takes its name from the pot, concave in shape to prevent the contents slopping over, in which it was cooked.

Among more elaborate feasts one worth recording was that given in 1623 by the Duke of Buckingham in his flagship off Santander, when he escorted the Prince of Wales (the future Charles I) to Madrid in fruitless pursuit of the hand of the Spanish *Infanta*. According to tradition, no less than 1600 dishes were served, and when the moment came for the sweets and the royal toast, the guns of the fleet fired a thunderous salute – resulting in the immediate destruction of the glass and crystal.

Merluza a la vasca (Basque-style hake), one of the best-known dishes from the region (recipe on page 136), is also one of the very few of which the origin and date are known. In his *Viaje por la cocina española*, Luis Antonio de la Vega recounts how he came upon a letter written during the first week of May 1723 by doña Placida de

Larrea of Bilbao to a namesake living in Navarra. Doña Plácida specifies that the fish must be caught from a small boat by hook and line and describes how she stewed it in an earthenware *cazuela* and served it with cockles and crabs in a green sauce made from parsley and with a garnish of asparagus, a present from friends in Tudela.

Basque fish dishes are so numerous that it is a question of picking out some of the best-known; they may be sampled at the Parador del Emperador in Fuenterrabía, installed in an historic castle across the estuary of the Bidassoa from Hendaye; in the Provincial Parador of Jaizkibel, high above the Atlantic; or in the many excellent restaurants of Bilbao and San Sebastián. Santander, although nominally in Old Castile, lies on the western fringe of the Basque country, of which its food is typical, notably the luscious *percebes*, a form of edible barnacle served as an apéritif; the spider crab, from which the meat is removed, cooked in white wine and replaced in the shell; or the homely but delicious fresh sardines, grilled over charcoal in the cafés flanking its wide beaches. A more ambitious restaurant, serving one of the best selection of *tapas* in the country, is the Riojano, stone-flagged and supported by great timber baulks, formerly a fisherman's *taberna*, but now atmospherically decorated with wine casks, the ends painted by some of the best artists in Spain. Its menu was designed by Picasso.

High on the list of fish recipes must come *bacalao a la vizcaina* (page 139). With its sauce containing garlic, red peppers, onion and breadcrumbs, this is a revelation to people who imagine that the salted and dried cod so popular in Spain and even more so in Portugal, is necessarily insipid. Inkfish is perhaps another specialized taste; it is at its best and most tender when cooked in a black sauce made from its own ink as *calamares en su tinta* (page 135). Prawns are often fried in a hot sauce made from chillis (*gambas al pil pil*, page 149). Other delicacies at their best in this region are *angulas* (page 134), the tiny freshwater eels, and *kokotxas* (page 137), a dish made from strips cut from the 'cheek' or throat of the hake. Since it takes a large number of hake to furnish sufficient of the *kokotxas*, you may find difficulty in obtaining it. Of better-known dishes, *paella marinera* (page 140) rewards eating.

The *Vascongadas* is also a region of mountains, divided from France by the Pyrenees and from the coast by the green, beech-carpeted Cantabrian mountains. It was at Burguete, near the Pass of Roncesvalles, that the hero of Ernest Hemingway's *The Sun Also Rises* fished trout from its cold streams; and rivers like the Deva, Nansa, Asón, Pas and Saja are renowned for their salmon. In season, the inn at Burguete is the headquarters for parties of sportsmen, who come from both sides of the frontier to shoot pigeon. They catch them also in the Pyrenean valleys, especially on the French side, by driving them up the steep defiles, one party of beaters advancing from the bottom and the others, stationed along the heights on either side, launching wooden batons in imitation of hawks, so as to keep the flock of pigeons low and direct it into a large net stretched across the top.

Among the wealth of fish, it is easy to forget that the Basque country also produces excellent beef, lamb and pork, and do not overlook the most individual *piperada* or Basque 'omelette' (also popular in the Basque region on the French side of the Pyrenees), made by breaking and stirring eggs into a purée of onions, tomatoes, peppers and chopped ham. This is one of the few parts of Spain where fresh cream is readily available and is used in making sweets. Incidentally it is a misconception that cream plays a significant part in the national cuisine. In southern Spain, what cream there is can only be bought in tins, largely produced by the Nestlé factory in Santander. The Basque cheeses, of which the best are the hard and semi-hard Gorbea, Orduña and Idiazabal, are made from ewe's milk.

Ninety per cent of the wine from the Vascongadas is from the southern fringe of the Province of Alava, over the mountains and geographically part of the Rioja. The Basque country proper produces only a thin 'green' wine, and that in very limited quantity, of which Richard Ford once wrote:

> Here also is made a poor wine called chacoli, Arabice chacalet, weakness, thinness; and the drink justifies the derivation, since it is far inferior to good Devonshire cider, and resembles those very ordinaire French wines *de Surenne* and *de Brie*. The Basques, from having nothing better, drink it copiously, and from the habit have even got to like it; however, it disagrees with the palate and the stomach of foreigners, who have not the dura Bascorum ilia . . .

Another Victorian traveller, Cyrus Redding, remarked disapprovingly that 'five or six different kinds of vines are engrafted in Biscay on one stock, which must render the wine of very dubious character'.

They were perhaps being a little unfair to Chacolí, a young, slightly *pétillant* wine, ready, like the 'green' wines of Galicia and Portugal, in the spring after the harvest. Chacolí may be either white or red (*txakoli gorri* and *txakoli zuri*). It is somewhat difficult to find in sophisticated restaurants and hotels, but drunk in Guernica, Guetaria and Zarauz, where the best of it is made, it can be a pleasant enough, though astringent, accompaniment to the magnificent shellfish.

Recipes

SALSA AL VINO BLANCO
WHITE WINE SAUCE
This is used for fish.

3 fl. oz (1 dl) dry white wine
4 shallots, chopped
3 egg yolks
3½ oz (100 g) butter
Salt
A little lemon juice

Put the white wine and shallots in a saucepan and simmer until the wine is reduced by half. Cool and strain through a sieve, then beat in the yolks one by one. Stand the saucepan in a *bain-marie* or vessel of boiling water and continue beating until the sauce thickens. Remove from the heat and immediately beat in the butter, in small pieces, a little salt and a few drops of lemon juice.

SALSA DE ACEITUNAS
OLIVE SAUCE
For fish.

2 oz (60 g) butter
1 small onion, chopped
1 tablespoon flour
½ glass chicken stock, made with a cube
1 teaspoon chopped parsley
½ glass sherry
½ lb (225 g) olives, stoned
Salt and pepper
Nutmeg

Heat half the butter in a pan, fry the chopped onion gently for 5 minutes, then add the flour and cook until it begins to brown. Now add the stock, parsley, sherry and olives and cook for another 3 or 4 minutes. Remove from the fire and beat in the remaining butter, finally seasoning the sauce with salt, pepper and nutmeg.

Salsa a la marinera
Fish sauce

A good accompaniment to grilled or baked fish. It is sometimes made with the addition of cooked peas.

Olive oil
1 onion, chopped
1 clove garlic, crushed
4 tomatoes, blanched and peeled
1 teaspoon sweet paprika powder
Salt
1 glass dry white wine
1 teaspoon flour
1 teacup water
2 fish heads
4 anchovies

Heat a little olive oil in a pan, fry the chopped onion until golden, drain off the oil and add the crushed garlic, tomatoes, paprika powder, a little salt and the glass of white wine. Allow to reduce by half, then mix in the flour with the cupful of cold water and stir it into the pan. Add the fish heads and anchovies and cook for 15 minutes or until there is only a little of the liquid left and the sauce is smooth. Strain through a sieve before using.

Mejillones con salsa marinera
Clams in fish sauce

Salsa marinera goes particularly well with clams. First scrape and wash them, then cover them with salted water in a saucepan. Bring to the boil and cook for 5 minutes. Now remove them with a draining spoon and take the fish from the shells. Keep the best half-shells, replace the cooked clams and pour the *salsa marinera* over them.

Ensalada de boquerones
Salad of fresh anchovies

Boquerones are in fact fresh anchovies. Their taste, when cooked and eaten fresh, bears little relation to that of the canned variety, being more like that of fresh sardines; they are delicious fried or grilled. When marinated according to the following recipe, they are served as an appetizer with drinks.

2 lb (1 kg) *boquerones*
Salt
1 tablespoon parsley, chopped
2 cloves garlic, chopped
Vinegar
2 tablespoons olive oil

Clean and wash the fish, removing the heads and backbones and opening them lengthwise. Season with salt, then put them in a deep glass dish in layers, sprinkling them with parsley and garlic, and covering them with vinegar and olive oil. Cover the dish and leave in the refrigerator for two days before serving.

Atun o bonito a la vinagreta
Tuna with vinaigrette sauce

2 lb (1 kg) fresh tuna, cut into 4 slices
2 small onions
2 cloves garlic, whole
Parsley, 1 sprig and a little chopped
1 bay leaf
Juice of ½ lemon
Freshly-ground white pepper
Salt
4 tablespoons olive oil
2 tablespoons vinegar
4 tomatoes, sliced

Clean and wash the fish, cover it with water in a saucepan and add one of the onions, the cloves of garlic, sprig of parsley, bay leaf, lemon juice and a little salt and pepper. Cook slowly for 10 minutes, allow it to cool in the water, then drain and transfer to a serving dish.

Chop the other onion and mix it well in a cup with the olive oil, vinegar, chopped parsley and a little salt and freshly-ground pepper. Pour this sauce over the fish and decorate with the slices of tomato.

Angulas en cazuela

These tiny freshwater eels, about the size of whitebait, are a great delicacy in the Basque region.

Per person:
A little olive oil
1 clove garlic, chopped
½ chilli, deseeded
5 oz (150 g) *angulas*

It is simplest to buy the *angulas* ready cooked, since their preparation is somewhat tedious; if you wish to start with fresh *angulas*, proceed as follows.

Buy a packet of black tobacco, used in Spain for rolling cigarettes, and stir rather less than 1 oz (20 g) in water. Add 1 lb (½ kg) *angulas* and stir with a wooden spoon until free of mucilage. Drain and rinse thoroughly in cold water. Meanwhile bring 3½ pints (2 litres) of salted water to the boil in a large saucepan. Add the *angulas*, stirring vigorously so that they do not stick together. Remove the saucepan from the fire, leave for 45 minutes, then strain off the water through a colander. The fish is now ready for further use.

Heat a little olive oil in individual *cazuelas* or fireproof casseroles, fry the chopped garlic briefly and add the chilli. Now stir in the *angulas* and cook for exactly 1 minute and no more. Cover and bring to the table sizzling hot.

Almejas de Fuenterrabia a la marinera
Clams Fuenterrabia style

2 lb (1 kg) clams
Olive oil
1 onion, chopped
1 teaspoon sweet paprika powder
4 tomatoes, blanched, peeled and chopped
1 small glass dry white wine
Salt and pepper
1 tablespoon chopped parsley

Wash the clams, scrape them with a knife and leave in cold water to get rid of sand. Heat the olive oil in a saucepan, fry the chopped onion for 10 minutes, then add the paprika powder and chopped tomatoes, moderating the heat so that they do not burn. Now stir in the clams, white wine and a little salt and pepper, and cook over a high flame until the clams open. Sprinkle with parsley and serve with slices of lemon.

Calamares en su tinta
Inkfish (squid) in their own ink

Along the Cantabrian coast inkfish are known as *chipirones* and the Basques have a traditional preference for those caught by rod and line and not in nets.

2 lb (1 kg) inkfish
Olive oil
2 onions, chopped
2 tomatoes, blanched, peeled and chopped
1 clove garlic, chopped
1 tablespoon chopped parsley
1 tablespoon fresh breadcrumbs
1 small glass brandy
Salt

Choose small inkfish, which are the most tender. Clean and cut them up as described on page 24, reserving the small ink bags and putting them in a little water so that they do not dry.

Heat the olive oil in a pan, fry the chopped onions until golden, then add the chopped tomatoes and cook gently for another 10 minutes. Stir in the prepared inkfish, add the chopped garlic, parsley, breadcrumbs and brandy and simmer for about 15 minutes. Now squeeze the ink from the sacs and add it to the contents of the pan, when the sauce will immediately turn a deep blue-black. Cook for another 10 minutes depending on the size of the inkfish; if they are large they will require longer.

Serve the inkfish in their sauce on a bed of boiled white rice.

Merluza a la vasca
Basque-style hake

A Basque recipe now famous throughout Spain.

4 slices hake
Flour
Olive oil
2 small onions, chopped
1 tablespoon chopped parsley
2 cloves garlic, crushed
1 tablespoon flour
2 dessertspoons fish stock or water
½ lb (225 g) garden peas, shelled and cooked
4 small boiled potatoes
Salt and pepper
8 asparagus tips
1 hard-boiled egg

First dredge the fish in flour, fry in hot olive oil until browned, then place in a saucepan.

Using the same olive oil, fry the chopped onions until golden, then add the parsley, crushed garlic and a tablespoon of flour, cook gently for 10 minutes, then stir in the fish stock or water. Pour this sauce over the fish in the saucepan, add the cooked peas, potatoes and a little salt and pepper, and cook together for 10 minutes until heated through. Serve on a dish garnished with the asparagus tips and wedges of hard-boiled egg.

Merluza con mahonesa y salsa de tomate
Hake with mayonnaise and tomato sauce

This dish is sometimes called *merluza Donostiarra* – the *Donst arros* being an alternative name for the Basques of the Cantabrian coast. The recipe may be used for any firm white fish.

2 lb (1 kg) hake or other firm white fish, in 1 piece
Salt and pepper
Juice of ½ lemon
1 oz (30 g) butter
½ pint (3 dl) *mahonesa verde* (see page 117)
½ pint (3 dl) *salsa de tomate* (see page 52)

Season the fish with salt and pepper, sprinkle with lemon juice and dot with butter, then wrap it up in cooking foil and bake in a medium oven (375° F/190° C/Mark 5) for ½ hour or a little longer, until the flesh comes away from the bones.

Allow the fish to cool in the foil, then take it out and open it carefully to remove the backbone and the smaller bones at the side. Close up the fish again and put it in an oven dish, pouring on to it first the green mayonnaise and then the tomato sauce. Return to the oven and bake for another 10 or 15 minutes. Sprinkle with parsley and serve with boiled potatoes.

The basic preparation may be done in the morning. If you have the mayonnaise and the tomato sauce ready, the fish may then be put in the oven for the final 10 or 15 minutes after the arrival of your guests.

KOKOTXAS DE MERLUZA

As described on page 129, these strips cut from the throat or 'cheek' of a hake are a great Basque delicacy.

A little olive oil
2 cloves garlic, chopped
1 tablespoon chopped parsley
7 oz (200 g) *kokotxas* per person

This dish is served from the individual earthenware *cazuelas* in which it is cooked – the small stove-enamelled French or Swedish pans made of heavy metal are a good alternative.

Heat a little olive oil, fry the chopped garlic and as soon as it changes colour add the parsley and *kokotxas*, shaking the *cazuela* so that they do not stick. They will be ready in 5 or 6 minutes and exude a little gelatinous liquid, which is the makings of the sauce.

Mero en salsa de almendras
Rock bass in almond sauce

A recipe which is equally good with other firm white fish.

2 lb (1 kg) rock bass or other firm white fish
Salt and pepper
1½ fl. oz (50 ml) olive oil
1 slice bread
1 clove garlic
1 sprig parsley
2 oz (60 g) almonds, shelled
1 small packet saffron
1 onion, chopped
1 lb (½ kg) tomatoes, blanched, peeled and chopped

Cut the fish into slices, season with salt and pepper, and put into a fish pan or metal oven dish.

Heat the olive oil in a pan, fry the bread, the clove of garlic, the parsley and almonds for a few minutes, then remove them with a draining spoon and transfer to a mortar. Add a little water and grind them into a smooth paste with the saffron.

Using the same oil and pan, fry the chopped onion and tomatoes for 10 to 15 minutes, then rub the mixture through a sieve or put it into a blender to make a purée. Mix this with the almond paste and pour it over the fish.

Heat the fish pan on top of the stove until the sauce begins to bubble, then put it into a preheated oven (375° F/190° C/Mark 5) and bake for about 30 minutes. Serve the fish from the container in which it has been cooked.

Gambas rebozadas
Crisp fried prawns in batter

2 lb (1 kg) prawns in shell
2 oz (50 g) sieved flour
1 tablespoon vinegar
Salt
1 white of egg, beaten stiff
Olive oil

If the prawns have not already been boiled, do so in salted water for 3 minutes, drain and leave them to cool, reserving the stock. Peel them, all but the tails, and put them on a plate.

Put the flour, vinegar and salt into a bowl and add 7 fl. oz (2 dl) of the fish stock little by little, stirring with a wooden spoon until the mixture thickens. Fold in the beaten egg white and mix well together.

Now heat the olive oil in a frying pan and when it begins to smoke, reduce the flame. Take the prawns by their tails, dip them into the batter and fry them in batches, taking care that they do not stick together (if you are using pre-cooked prawns and have no stock, use water instead and dip them into the batter with a spoon).

Finally, take the prawns from the frying pan with a slotted spoon and drain off excess oil on kitchen paper before serving.

Bacalai a la vizcaina
Bacalao Biscay style

The classic Spanish method of cooking *bacalao*. This dried and salted cod may be obtained in most countries in specialized food stores and delicatessens.

2 lb (1 kg) *bacalao*
Flour
Olive oil
2 chillis, soaked
2 cloves garlic
1 slice fried bread
½ pint (3 dl) *salsa española* (see page 52)
1 tablespoon chopped parsley
2 oz (60 g) breadcrumbs
2 red peppers, blanched, deseeded and cut into strips

Cut the *bacalao* into pieces and soak them overnight. Next morning drain them, immerse in fresh water and bring to boiling point, then remove and drain the fish. Take out the bones, dredge in flour and fry in hot olive oil until golden.

Grind the chillis, garlic and fried bread in a mortar, stir this paste into the *salsa española* and pour half of the mixture into an oven dish. Lay the pieces of *bacalao* in the sauce, then pour the other half over them. Sprinkle the surface with chopped parsley and breadcrumbs, garnish with the strips of red pepper, and bake in a medium oven (375° F/190° C/Mark 5) for 15 minutes.

Paella marinera

As already explained, a *paella marinera* is one made solely from fish, without the addition of chicken or meat. If you are camping or staying in an apartment on the Cantabrian coast, this is an opportunity to visit the local market and buy all the assorted fish for a truly magnificent *paella* (see recipe, page 38).

Piperada vasca
Basque omelette

This is not a true omelette, but is made in basically the same way as *huevos revueltos*. With its varied ingredients it is a fairly substantial supper dish.

A little olive oil
2 onions, chopped
4 fresh red peppers, deseeded and cut into strips, or the contents of an 8 oz (225 g) can of peppers
4 tomatoes, blanched, skinned and chopped
4 oz (110 g) bacon or 4 slices cooked ham
Salt
Freshly-ground black pepper
1 or 2 eggs per person

Heat a little olive oil in a large frying pan, cook the chopped onions and strips of red pepper for 10 or 15 minutes until the onions are golden, then drain off the oil. If canned peppers are used, they should not be fried with the onions, but added now, together with the chopped tomatoes and bacon, a little salt and the freshly-ground black pepper. Cook these ingredients together for about 5 minutes, then pour the lightly-beaten eggs into the pan and stir vigorously with a wooden spoon until the mixture sets.

When slices of cooked ham are used instead of bacon, they should be served on top of the *piperada*.

Lomo de cerdo al estilo vasco
Loin of pork Basque style

2 lb (1 kg) loin of pork
Salt
1 clove garlic, peeled
2 oz (60 g) pork fat
5 fl. oz (150 ml) milk
Pepper

Season the meat with salt and rub it with garlic. Now heat the pork fat in a stewpan over a high heat and brown the outside of the joint. Add the milk and some pepper and cook slowly for 1 hour or until the meat is tender.

Asturias and Galicia

Galicia, in the far north-west of Spain, and Asturias on its eastern border, are as rich in culinary resources as the Basque country; and even the critical Alexandre Dumas favoured Galicia with a few words of commendation:

> It is in Galicia that one eats the best fish, particularly fresh cod, eels, both from the rivers or the sea, lamprey and finally octopus, a species of squid [*sic*] which is the food of the poor. There are good clams; here you will find oysters, plumper and less salty than from the sea, like those from the lagoons of Naples. It is the only place where they are marinated and despatched all over Europe in barrels [this before air transport and refrigeration made it possible to send them to Madrid for sale the same day].
>
> France abounds in truffles, Castile in olives, Catalonia in plums and Galicia in chestnuts . . . in *marron glacé*, the most exquisite confection known to the civilized world . . .

He was so impressed by *caldo gallego*, a rich meat and vegetable *potage*, that he took the recipe back to France, but could not resist a parting tilt at Castile:

> The difference between the Castilian and the Galician is that the Castilian subsists on bread, cheese and chick-peas, and the Galician on bread made of maize or rye and on greens. We cannot say whether it is the diet or climate which makes them so different; the Galician is straightforward, hospitable and polite, both to his own folk and to foreigners; whereas the Castilian is quarrelsome, off-hand, inhospitable and proud, and has no use for the French or even Spaniards from other provinces.

Probably because of the mountainous terrain and wet climate, which had little appeal to the invaders from North Africa, Galicia and the Asturias were the one part of the country never to be occupied by the Moors – and proved to be their Achilles heel. It was King Pelayo of Asturias who, according to legend, defeated a Moorish army at Covadonga in 718, so striking a first blow in the centuries-long Reconquest, during the early stages of which his successors were to play the leading role. On a gastronomic note, his son, Fávila, suffered an untimely death in a struggle with a bear, apparently through disregarding his father's advice to build up his strength with a daily dish of *fabes* (or broad beans).

During the Middle Ages Galicia became the spiritual rallying point for the hard-pressed Christians. According to legend Santiago de Compostela (*campus stellae* or 'the field of the star') was the furthest point reached by St James the Apostle in his missionary travels and his remains are buried there. The defeat of the omnipotent 'Abd-al-Rahman III at Simancas in 939 was attributed to the miraculous intervention of the saint on the field of battle, and from the eleventh century the pilgrimage to his shrine was the most famous in Europe. After the Benedictines from Cluny built a cathedral to house the shrine and constructed staging points along the route from France, the pilgrimage formed the single most important link between Spain and Christian Europe, and the Cluniacs and their Burgundian confrères were later to play a leading part in the emergence of an independent Portugal.

The cockle shells, worn as a badge by the pilgrims, are commemorated today in the name of the well-known Galician dish, *conchas de peregrino*, somewhat akin to the French *coquilles St Jacques*. The Hotel Reyes Católicos, installed in a sixteenth-century palace in the magnificent cathedral square in Santiago, is incidentally known throughout Spain for the high standard of its cooking.

Much later in Spain's history, the far north was to play a crucial role in organizing resistance to another invader. In May 1808 the Supreme Junta of Asturias sent deputies to London with an urgent plea for help in the struggle against Napoleon. It was this overture from the Asturians which first set in motion British intervention in the Peninsular War; and La Coruña at the northernmost tip of Galicia was the end-point of the tragic retreat, which culminated in the death of Sir John Moore and the evacuation of the British expeditionary force during the early stages of the war.

Perhaps the best introduction to the regional cooking is to take the long road from Santander through Asturias and then down into Galicia. After leaving Gijón, surprisingly the largest port in Spain, and passing the huge steel mills of that Asturian Sheffield, Avilés, the route winds among the hills and apple orchards, eventually emerging on to a green coastal strip between the snow-capped mountains and the rocky coves of the Atlantic coast.

The best-known dish of these parts is *fabada asturiana*, a nourishing stew made with a basis of *alubias* or dry white beans (the Asturians maintain that a good *fabada* can only be made with the beans from the province) and *morcilla*, the local blood sausage, of which the nearest British equivalent is the Scottish black pudding, and a variety of other ingredients. There are numerous restaurants in Oviedo, the capital of the province, which make a good *fabada*; another, to be recommended for a representative selection of well-cooked regional specialities, including the attractive *sopa de avellanas* (hazelnut soup with croûtons, see the recipe on page 148), *merluza a la sidra* (hake in a sauce made from cider, brandy, mussels, flour, hard-boiled eggs and red peppers) and *arroz requemado asturiana* (a particularly delicious form of milky rice pudding, flavoured with aniseed, cinnamon and lemon, and topped with brittle caramel), is the Parador del Molino Viejo in Gijón.

Asturias produces no wine, but makes the best cider in Spain, formerly drunk from the barrel, but now bottled and aerated and sent both to other parts of Spain and abroad. The best-known brand, 'El Gaitero', is considerably more expensive than wine. Cider is often used to advantage in Asturias for cooking fish, and parallels have been drawn with the cider-producing areas of Normandy and Brittany in France.

Another speciality is the blue cheese from Cabrales, reminiscent of Roquefort and indeed so fully flavoured that there is a *canard* that it is matured in heaps of manure! This is, of course, quite untrue. The curd is first skimmed from the whey with a hollow circle of bark like that used by the Homeric Greeks and then dried in front of a fire. It is subsequently transferred to an *horreo* (from the Latin *horreum*), a wooden shed on stone stilts, typical of Asturias and Galicia and used generally to store grain away from the damp or rats. When the blue mould makes its appearance the cheeses are taken to the famous cave of Jouz del Cuevu to complete their maturation among the great stalactites, and must be eaten within a few weeks after being removed from the cave.

Cabrales is not the only cheese from Asturias. Also made from cow's milk, sometimes with the addition of ewe's or goat's milk, is the very similar Gamonedo; while the Queso de los Bellos is hard and made from ewe's milk. Galicia, too, makes cheeses in some variety, all from cow's milk, the main types being the hard or semi-hard Cebrero and San Simón, and the soft Tetilla and Ulloa for immediate consumption.

Over the mountain border with Galicia, the scenery changes and gives way to granite mountains, falling away towards the coast to the myriad *Rías*, greatly resembling the fjords of Norway. The best time to visit Galicia is in the early summer, when the rain relents, and its mountain slopes, fragrant with pine and eucalyptus and strewn with flowers, are a vast natural rock garden.

The waters of the *Rías* are the source of much of Galicia's splendid shellfish. Particularly interesting is that of the great Atlantic seaport of Vigo. Upstream of the harbour the blue waters of the estuary, with their green mountain backdrop, are dotted with what at first appear to be small black houseboats, but are in fact *mejilloneras* or floating platforms for fishing cultured mussels. These are, of course, only one of the numerous varieties of *mariscos*, which include lobsters, scallops, prawns and scampi in all shapes and sizes; clams, cockles, oysters, *percebes* (an edible barnacle resembling a detached clump of lobster's claws) and *nécoras* (a species of spider crab). All of this magnificent assemblage may be eaten (at a price) in the shellfish bars or *marisquerías*, where they are now sold by weight. The white fish, too, is among the best in Spain.

Among the best of the Galician fish dishes is the *caldereta de pescado* (page 152), a rich fish stew, almost identical with the *caldeirada* from across the frontier – there are many resemblances between the cooking of Galicia and that of northern Portugal – and with a strong family likeness to *bouillabaisse*. This northern part of the Peninsula was once an historical whole, and links with Portugal are again evident in the *caldo a la gallega*, a soup with a strong affinity to the famous *caldo verde* of the Minho, or in *callos a la gallega*, in which tripe is highly spiced and served with haricot beans in the style of the justly famous *tripas à modo do Porto*. The *empanada gallega* (page 154), a thick tart with a filling of onions, tomatoes and peppers, together with sardines or loin of pork, is very characteristic of Galicia, as is *lacón con grelos*, ham bones cooked with *chorizo* and sprouting turnip tops. All of this is hearty but extremely appetizing fare, appropriate to the cold and wet winters. There are some good sweets, including *filloas* (page 158), cream-filled pancakes cooked in liqueur, and *flan de manzanas* (page 156), a variation on the baked cream caramel so universally popular in Spain, made with apple purée.

Apart from Santiago de Compostela, the most important cities of Galicia are La Coruña, Lugo, Vigo and Pontevedra, where you will have no difficulty in finding these dishes, or such popular favourites as *paella* and *zarzuela* or simple grilled meat, which is of excellent quality. The Paradores also serve local dishes; the best regional menu is that of the remote Condes de Villalba to the north.

It may be surprising that Galicia, with its wet winters and short summers, is one of the largest wine-producing areas in Spain. That its wines, so similar to the *vinhos verdes* or 'green wines' of northern Portugal, are not better-known abroad is probably because they would not travel until modern methods were introduced for stabilizing them. They were certainly much drunk by John of Gaunt's soldiers in 1386, when, as Froissart records in his *Chronicle*, the English army was incapacitated for two days, and were also the bane of Sir John Moore's troops during the retreat to La Coruña; his half-tipsy troops were cut down in droves by the pursuing French dragoons.

The hard-working and inventive Galicians found an answer to their wet climate by training the vines clear of the damp ground on tall granite pillars. This results in the grapes receiving less reflected sunshine than those grown low as in other parts of the country; and the wine would be unacceptably sharp but for a specialized secondary fermentation, which, as in the Portuguese Minho, eliminates most of the malic acid present in the unripe fruit.

The so-called *vinos verdes* may in fact be either white or red and are ready for drinking in the late spring following the harvest. The red wine, though much appreciated by Galicians, is generally too tart for foreign palates. The whites, on the other hand, are delicate and flowery and often display a *pétillance* or slight tingle on the tongue. They have sometimes been compared to Moselles; and there is in fact good reason to believe that vines were brought to Galicia from the Rhine and Moselle by the Cluniac monks in the twelfth century.

The Galician wine most easily available, both in the region itself and in other parts of Spain, is 'Pazo' – the word means a seignorial residence, of which a fine example is the Parador at Pontevedra – made at the great cooperative at Ribadavia, west of Orense on the River Miño near the Portuguese frontier. There is an old rhyme which runs:

Si queres tratarme ben
dame vino do Ribeiro,
pan trigo de Ribadavia,
nenas do chan de Amoeiro
[If you wish to do me well
Give me wine from Ribeiro,
Wheaten bread from Ribadavia
And girls from Amoeiro].

Of the different wines made by the cooperative, the white 'Pazo' is delicate, dry and fruity, only very slightly *pétillant* and an excellent accompaniment to shellfish. The *rosado* (rosé), light and refreshing, possesses a more definite sparkle, while the red is a brusque wine, dry to the point of acidity and perhaps best left to Galicians and *aficionados*. In common with other 'green wines', none of them contains more than about 10° to 12° of alcohol. All are stabilized by refrigeration.

Valdeorras to the north and Verín and Monterrey to the east make stronger red wines, sometimes grown low – *a la castellana*, as they say in Galicia.

The best of the white Galician wine is made from the Albariño grape – just as the best of the Portuguese *vinhos verdes* are the Alvarinhos from Monçao across the River Miño (or Minho, in its Portuguese form). Production centres on the area around Cambados, north of Pontevedra and opposite the Island of La Toja, where an annual Fiesta del Albariño is held in August and the wines from different growers may be sampled. The most famous, the Fefiñanes Palacio, actually made in the Palace of Fefiñanes on the outskirts of Cambados by the Marqués de Figueroa, is not strictly a 'green' wine, since it is aged in oak casks for several years, by which time it has lost its sparkle. More typical is the Albariño del Palacio, made by his brother, definitely *pétillant* and astonishingly fresh and flowery. It may be obtained at the charming Parador de Cambados, with its eucalyptus-shaded garden, and like other Galician wines, both red and white, should be drunk stone-cold.

It is not normal in Spain for brandy and spirits to be made in the same establishments as wine, but the Bodega Cooperativa del Ribeiro produces a very potent *aguardiente*, akin to the French *marc de Bourgogne* or Portuguese *bagaceira*, by distilling the skins and pips of the grapes. It is often drunk from white chinaware bowls (also used for the red wine) and is first set alight to burn off some of the plentiful alcohol. In this form it is known as *queimada*, from the Spanish *quemar*, 'to burn'. More elaborate *queimadas* are prepared by pouring a bottle or half-bottle of *aguardiente* into a large earthenware *cazuela*, adding slices of lemon, roast coffee beans and maraschino cherries and setting alight the brew – leaving plenty of headroom for the resulting blaze. The grateful liquid is then ladled out into glasses. Without going to Galicia, you may obtain a good *queimada* at any of the Galician restaurants in Madrid; and most cheering it is on a cold winter's day.

Recipes

SOPA DE AVELLANAS
HAZELNUT SOUP

½ pint (3 dl) chicken stock
2 oz (60 g) toasted breadcrumbs
1 small packet saffron
1 clove garlic
2 oz (60 g) hazelnuts
Salt and pepper

Warm the stock in a saucepan and stir in the breadcrumbs to make a smooth cream. Grind the saffron, garlic and nuts and add the paste to the broth. Season with salt and pepper and simmer for 10 minutes.

HABAS A LA ASTURIANA
BROAD BEANS ASTURIAN STYLE

¼ pint (1½ dl) olive oil
5 oz (150 g) chopped ham or bacon
1 clove garlic, chopped
1 teaspoon sweet paprika powder
2 lb (1 kg) shelled broad beans
3 carrots, scraped and sliced
1 glass dry white wine
1 pint approx. (½ litre) stock
Salt and pepper
4 small new potatoes or 1 old potato, peeled and cut up.

Heat the olive oil in a saucepan, fry the ham or bacon and the chopped garlic for a minute or two, then stir in the paprika powder and remove from the fire. Add the broad beans, carrots, wine, stock, and a little salt and pepper, and bring to the boil. Now reduce the heat, put the lid on the saucepan and simmer for 45 minutes. Add the potatoes and cook slowly for another ½ hour.

Tortilla a la asturiana
Asturian omelette

A full-flavoured omelette in the shape of a pancake and substantial enough for a main dish.

Olive oil
2 oz (60 g) minced veal
2 shallots or 1 small onion, chopped
4 tomatoes, blanched, peeled and chopped
2 canned red peppers, cut up
8 eggs
2 oz (60 g) grated cheese
Salt and pepper

Heat a little olive oil in a frying pan and cook the minced meat with the chopped shallots for 10 minutes. Drain off and reserve the oil, then add the tomatoes and peppers and cook together for another 5 minutes. Meanwhile beat the eggs in a bowl, add the contents of the frying pan and also the grated cheese and a little salt and pepper.

Now return the pan to the fire with the reserved oil, and once it begins to smoke pour in the egg mixture and cook until golden-brown on the under side. Place a plate on top of the pan and invert the omelette on to it. Without adding more oil, slide back the omelette and leave it for another minute or two to brown the uncooked side. Serve hot from the fire.

Gambas al pil pil
Prawns with chillis

Gambas al pil pil are served as an appetizer with fresh bread to dunk in the sauce. It is an *extremely* hot dish – if you find the chillis too fiery, remove the seeds before cooking them.

2 lb (1 kg) prawns in shell or 8 oz (225 g) frozen prawns
Olive oil
3 cloves garlic, crushed
2 chillis, chopped

If the prawns are in shell, first peel them. Heat a little olive oil in individual *cazuelas* or fireproof dishes, then add the crushed garlic, chopped chillis and prawns and fry briefly. Serve smoking hot from the stove.

Vieiras gallegas
Scallops Galician style

8 scallops
4 oz (110 g) butter
Salt and pepper
Juice of 1 lemon
2 tablespoons chopped parsley

Remove the scallops from the shells and keep these warm in a low oven for serving the fish.

Heat the butter in a saucepan until it darkens, season the scallops with salt and pepper and cook slowly for about 10 minutes. Add the lemon juice, cook for a little longer, then sprinkle in some of the chopped parsley, shaking the pan. Put back the scallops in the shells and serve with all speed.

Merluza a la gallega
Hake Galician style

Cod, halibut and other firm white fish may also be cooked in this way.

4 slices hake
Salt
Thyme
1 bay leaf
Parsley, 1 sprig and a little chopped
Olive oil
Vinegar
1 onion cut into rings
2 cloves garlic, chopped
4 potatoes, peeled and sliced
1 tablespoon sweet paprika powder

Simmer the hake in salted water for 10 minutes with the thyme, bay leaf, sprig of parsley and a little olive oil and vinegar.

Meanwhile heat a little olive oil in a pan, fry the onion rings for 5 minutes and before they change colour add the garlic and chopped parsley and the sliced potatoes. Cook for another 5 minutes, adding a little water from the fish – but the sauce should remain thick.

Now put the fish on a serving dish and arrange the slices of potato and rings of onion around it. Add a little more olive oil, the paprika and a few drops of vinegar to the sauce in the pan. Heat very briefly, since it will otherwise blacken, and pour over the fish.

The highly-cured *jamones serranos*, the best of which come from the west of Spain, are a familiar sight in bars all over the country

Above An *horreo* at Tuy near the Portuguese frontier for storing grain or maturing cheeses safe from damp or vermin

Below Trellised vines at the Palace of Fefiñanes in Galicia. The grapes make a 'green wine' with a slight sparkle

Above A peasant in traditional costume with silver buttons at the mediaeval village of La Alberca near Ciudad Rodrigo

Below Not so long ago La Alberca was without electricity. Cooking the evening meal at the local *fonda* (inn) over an open fire

The Roman Theatre at Mérida, once the headquarters of the legions which policed western Spain and Portugal

Sardinas a la asturiana
Sardines Asturian style

This dish is very popular with the fishermen of the Cantabrian coast, who cook it on their boats. When it is made at home, it is the man, not his wife, who cooks it.

4 oz (120 g) pork fat
5 oz (150 g) tomatoes, blanched, peeled and chopped
1 onion, chopped
2 lb (1 kg) fresh sardines, cleaned and washed
4 cloves garlic, chopped
1 chilli, deseeded and chopped
1 glass dry white wine
Salt and pepper
2 bay leaves

Heat half of the pork fat in a pan and fry the chopped tomatoes, then add the onion and cook gently for a further 10 minutes. Put the rest of the pork fat into an oven dish and arrange the sardines on the bottom in two layers. Pour the onion and tomato sauce over them and sprinkle on the other ingredients in the order given. Cover the dish and bake in a very moderate oven (325° F/170° C/Mark 3) for ½ hour.

Lubina a la asturiana
Bass with mussels or clams Asturian style

This recipe also works well with other firm white fish.

1 bass of about 2 lb (1 kg) cut into slices
Salt
A little olive oil
1 glass dry white wine
1 teaspoon sweet paprika powder
1 onion, chopped
2 doz mussels or clams, scraped and washed
Chopped parsley

Season the slices of fish with salt, arrange them in an oven dish and sprinkle them with a little olive oil, the white wine, paprika powder and chopped onion. Put the dish into a moderate preheated oven (350° F/180° C/Mark 4) and bake for about ½ hour (the fish is done when the bones come away from the flesh).

Meanwhile boil the mussels or clams in salted water until they open. Remove the fish from the shells, keeping the best half-shells and replacing the cooked mussels or clams in them. Take the dish from the oven and arrange the half-shells around it. Sprinkle with parsley before bringing to the table.

Caldeirada gallega
Galician fish stew

Like the Portuguese dish of the same name or the French *bouillabaisse*, this is served in two parts: first the broth with slices of toast, and then the fish.

Either: 8 oz (225 g) angler fish
8 oz (225 g) hake
8 oz (225 g) rock bass
Or: 1½ lb (675 g) assorted firm white fish
7 oz (200 g) prawns in shell
3 fl. oz (1 dl) olive oil
¾ oz (20 g) flour
2 medium-sized onions, chopped
2 cloves garlic, crushed
1 tablespoon chopped parsley
1 bay leaf
Salt
Freshly-ground white pepper
4 slices toast

Clean the fish and cut it up, then marinate it for 2 hours in a mixture of the olive oil, flour, chopped onion, crushed garlic and parsley, and the bay leaf. Now put the fish in a saucepan, season with salt and pepper, add 1½ pints (1 litre) of cold water and bring to the boil. Cook very slowly for 15 minutes, adding the prawns towards the end.

Serve the broth with the toast floating on it.

Empanada gallega
Savoury tart from Galicia

Serves 6. Perhaps the best-known of Galician dishes, this tart may contain either meat or fish, often sardines.

Pastry

10 oz (300 g) flour, sieved
1 oz approx. (20 g) dried yeast
1 egg, beaten
2½ oz (75 g) pork fat or butter
2 fl. oz (50 ml) milk

Filling

2 fl. oz (50 ml) olive oil
1 onion, chopped
3½ oz (100 g) tomatoes, blanched, peeled and chopped
2 canned red peppers, cut into strips
7 oz (200 g) ham or *chorizo*, diced

Put 3 oz (90 g) of flour into a bowl, making a well in the centre. Dissolve the yeast in 3 tablespoons of warm water, pour it into the flour and knead with the fingers to make a smooth and compact ball of dough. Transfer this to a large bowl filled with warm water. To begin with the dough will sink to the bottom, but as the yeast works on it, it will grow lighter and rise to the surface; it is then ready.

Put the rest of the flour into another bowl, add the beaten egg (reserving a little to paint the dough in the final stages), the pork fat or butter and the milk. Knead into a smooth dough, then combine the two masses of dough, flouring your fingers and working the mixture thoroughly until it forms a single smooth and compact whole. Cover with a clean tea towel or leave in a bowl with a plastic lid and allow to rest in a warm place for 1 hour.

Meanwhile make the filling. Heat a little olive oil in a pan, fry the chopped onion until golden and drain off the oil. Now stir in the chopped tomatoes and strips of pepper, cook for a few minutes more and add the diced ham or *chorizo*, or a mixture of both. Having stirred all the ingredients well, allow the mixture to cool on a plate preparatory to filling.

Grease a flat baking tray, then divide the dough into equal parts and roll them out to size on a pastry board or marble slab. Use one of the pieces to line the tin and spread out the filling on it. Place the other sheet of dough on top, cut round it, seal the edges and paint with the reserved beaten egg. Preheat the oven to 350°–375° F/180°–190° C/Mark 4–5 and bake for 20 to 30 minutes until the pastry is golden.

Instead of ham or *chorizo* you may use either fried fresh or canned sardines, which are added to the sauce at the appropriate point; and in place of making the pastry, the lazy way out – which nevertheless gives acceptable results – is to buy ready-prepared puff pastry.

Conejo a la asturiana
Rabbit in cider Asturian style

2 large potatoes
2 large turnips
2 large carrots
3½ oz (100 g) butter
1 oz (25 g) pine kernels
Liver of the rabbit
1 tablespoon flour
1½ pints (1 litre) cider
5 oz (150 g) fresh belly of pork, finely chopped
2 onions, finely chopped
1 rabbit large enough for 4, cleaned and cut up
Salt and pepper

Peel and cut up the potatoes, turnips and carrots, then heat half of the butter in a pan and fry the vegetables for about 10 minutes. Meanwhile mince the pine kernels and liver in a 'Mouli' or grind them in a mortar. Mix the flour in a cup with a little cider and stir the paste, together with the minced liver and pine kernels, into the pan with the vegetables.

Now melt the rest of the butter in a stewpan, fry the chopped belly of pork and chopped onions for 10 minutes, then add the rabbit, seasoning it with salt and pepper, and the contents of the frying pan. Cover the rabbit with the rest of the cider and cook slowly for an hour or two until tender. The time will depend on its size.

FARINES O FARRAPES
CORNMEAL PORRIDGE

The winters in Asturias are cold and wet, as they are in Scotland, and this 'porridge' was traditionally eaten for breakfast. It is made, not with cornflour, but with a coarser yellow cornmeal made by milling maize.

Per person:
1 breakfast cup water
Pinch of salt
1¼ oz (35 g) cornmeal
Knob of butter

Bring a saucepan of water to the boil, adding a pinch of salt. Pour a little cold water into a bowl and stir the cornmeal into it, so as to make a smooth paste. Add this to the boiling water, stirring vigorously with a wooden spoon to begin with, so that it does not stick to the bottom of the pan. Now simmer gently for about 2 hours with occasional stirring. Finally incorporate a knob of unsalted butter.

It is served in a bowl with a cup of milk on the side, and the traditional way of eating it is to take a spoonful and then dip it in the milk.

FLAN DE MANZANAS
CARAMELIZED APPLE FLAN

3 heaped tablespoons caster sugar
2 lb (1 kg) cooking apples, peeled and cut up
3 tablespoons brown sugar
1 cinnamon stick
A little lemon peel
3 egg yolks

First caramelize the caster sugar by heating it in a small saucepan with a teaspoonful of water. Coat the bottom of a flan dish and leave to cool.

Now put the cut-up apples into a saucepan with 3 tablespoons of water, the brown sugar, cinnamon stick and a twist of lemon peel. Cook until the apple is soft, then rub the mixture through a sieve to make a smooth purée. Beat in the three egg yolks, pour into the caramel-coated mould, and cook in a *bain-marie* for about ¾ hour. This may be done either in a moderate oven or on top of the stove. To test whether the flan is cooked, push in a cooking knife or large needle; if it comes out clean, the flan is done. Leave to cool and invert on to a serving dish.

Croquetas de manzana
Apple croquettes

1 lb 10 oz (750 g) cooking apples, peeled and cut up
1 vanilla pod
4½ oz (125 g) sugar
1 dessertspoon potato flour
1 oz (25 g) butter
4 egg yolks
Breadcrumbs
Olive oil
Icing sugar

Boil the cut-up apple in ½ pint (250 ml) of water with the vanilla pod and sugar and, when soft, strain and rub it through a sieve. Return the apple purée to the saucepan, stir in the potato flour and butter and cook very slowly for another 10 minutes until the mixture thickens. Allow it to cool and then blend with the egg yolks. Shape the croquettes with a couple of dessertspoons, dredge them in breadcrumbs and fry in hot olive oil until golden. Sprinkle them with icing sugar and serve hot.

Diablillos rellenos
Jam pasties

9 oz (250 g) puff pastry
Apricot jam
Olive oil
Icing sugar

Roll out the pastry into circles of about 3 inches (7 cm) in diameter and put a spoonful of apricot or other jam in the centre of each. Fold around and seal the edges with a fork, then fry in hot olive oil for about 10 minutes until golden. Remove any excess oil on kitchen paper and sprinkle with icing sugar before serving.

Tortilla soplada al limon
Lemon souffle omelette

4 eggs
Pinch of salt
3½ oz (100 g) caster sugar
Peel of 1 lemon, grated
Butter
Icing sugar

Separate the whites and yolks of the eggs. Add a pinch of salt to the whites and beat stiff, then beat the yolks in a separate bowl with the sugar and grated lemon peel. Now blend the mixtures with a wooden spoon and pour carefully into an oven dish greased with a little butter. Powder with icing sugar and cook in a hot oven (425° F/220° C/Mark 7) for 5 minutes.

Serve immediately.

Filloas
Sweet pancakes

In Galicia these thick, fluffy pancakes are usually rolled and filled with jam and sprinkled with caster sugar. They are also delicious when served flat and topped with caramel or grenadine syrup and whipped cream.

To make 6 filloas:
4 oz (110 g) flour
Pinch of salt
1 egg
½ pint (3 dl) milk

Sieve the flour and salt into a basin. Make a well in the centre, drop in the egg and add half of the milk little by little, stirring with a wooden spoon to make a smooth batter. Beat with a whisk to break up lumps, then incorporate the rest of the milk and allow to rest for 20 minutes.

Grease a small omelette pan, heat until it begins to smoke and add 3 or 4 tablespoons of the batter, shaking the pan so that it spreads out evenly. Cook rapidly until the pancake is golden underneath and bubbly on top, then turn it with a palette knife and cook on the other side.

Extremadura

The Extramadura, from the Latin *Extrema Ora*, lies on the western extreme of Spain bordering Portugal. A region of rolling sierras, cork oaks and wandering flocks of sheep and pigs, it was largely depopulated after the Reconquest, when its inhabitants, among them Cortés and Pizarro, swelled the ranks of the Conquistadors who sought their fortunes in Spanish America.

In Roman times Augusta Emerita, the present Mérida, was the capital of Lusitania, which also embraced most of modern Portugal, the headquarters of Augustus' legions and the ninth city of the Empire. Many of its Roman remains still survive, including the magnificent theatre, an amphitheatre and vestiges of a circus, an aqueduct, the great bridge across the River Guadiana and a triumphal arch of Trajan.

After its reconquest from the Moors by Alfonso IX of Léon in 1228, the prosperity of the area declined; and the repositories of culture and cuisine were the great monasteries of Alcántara, Guadalupe and Yuste. Something has already been said about Alcántara's contribution to gastronomy and of the pillage of its recipe books by General Junot during the preliminaries to the Peninsular War (see page 6). Guadalupe, in the mountains on the eastern fringe of the Extremadura, owed its foundation to the unearthing of a statue of the Virgin, buried during the Moorish conquest, towards the end of the thirteenth century. The Virgin of Guadalupe subsequently became the patron saint of the Conquistadors; the monastery was frequented by generations of Spanish monarchs, including the Reyes Católicos – it was here that they authorized Columbus to undertake his first voyage of discovery – and soon rivalled Santiago de Compostela as the object of pilgrimage. In his *Grandezas de España* of 1549 Pedro de Medina lists the annual fare provided by the ecclesiastical authorities for the sustenance of these pilgrims. It ran to some fifteen thousand bushels of wheat; fifty thousand gallons of wine; and six or seven thousand head of cattle, in addition to veal, kids, chicken and game.

Despite its sack by Napoleon's troops, the monastery is still a storehouse of treasures. The series of scenes from the life of St Jerome, painted for its sacristy, are among Zurbarán's finest works; the wooden image of the Virgin, blackened by the kisses of countless pilgrims, still survives, as do its marvellous collections of jewelled vestments and illustrated choir books.

The monastery of Yuste, on the southern slopes of the Sierra de Gredos, will always be associated with Charles V, who spent his last years there after abdicating as Holy Roman Emperor in 1555 and relinquishing the Spanish throne in the same year. Charles was a celebrated trencherman, as appears from his description by the Spanish historian Emilio Castelar:

> He had a voracious appetite and was always hungry. Through eating so much he suffered, if not from indigestion, from stomach disorders, aggravated by the structure of his jaw [Castelar is referring to the well-known hereditary defect of the Hapsburgs] and the complete impossibility of chewing his food. However, he in no way modified his eating habits after his retirement . . .
>
> The mail coaches from Lisbon to Valladolid went far out of their way to deliver fish to Yuste, and the *Corregidor* of Placencia received the strictest orders from Valladolid to provide the Emperor with all the meat he demanded. . . . Suffice it to say that Valladolid presented him with eel pies, Zaragoza with veal, Ciudad Real with game, Gama with partridge, Denia with sausages, Cadiz with anchovies, Seville with oysters, Lisbon with sole, the Extremadura with olives, Toledo with marzipans and Guadalupe with stews devised by its numerous and inventive chefs.

To deal with this mountain of provisions, a stove was installed in the monastery, of such dimensions that all sixty of the Emperor's servants could gather round it and warm themselves at the same moment.

Because of its proximity to Portugal, the main base for Wellington's armies during the Peninsular War, the Extremadura was a cockpit for pitched battles between the two sides – names like Talavera, Badajoz, Albuera and Medellín have passed into military history. The area was stripped of its resources and its great monasteries were sacked and declined from their former glory; but if the Extremadura can no longer boast culinary profusion, it still furnishes a variety of interesting regional dishes. Among these are *gazpacho extremeño*, a variant on the cold soups so popular in

Andalusia; *bacalao al estilo monacal* (salt cod monasterial style), described by Dionisio Pérez as a 'delicious mortification for a day of fast'; a variety of roasts and stews of lamb and kid; stuffed pheasant and partridge pie; excellent trout and, of course, numerous sweets traditionally made in the convents.

But the glory of the Extremadura is its pork. Other places in Spain, such as Jabugo and Trevélez, are noted for their *jamón serrano*. There can scarcely be a region in the northern part of the country which does not make its own variety of *chorizo* or cured sausage, but in *embutidos* (or *charcuterie*) the Extremadura is so pre-eminent that it seems appropriate to quote unashamedly and at length from the old master, Richard Ford:

> The killing takes place about the 10th and 11th of November . . . and the death of a fat pig is as great an event in Spanish families, who generally fatten one up, as the birth of a baby; nor can the fact be kept secret, so audible is his announcement. It is considered a delicate attention on the part of the proprietor to celebrate the auspicious event by sending a portion of the chitterlings to intimate friends . . .
>
> The capital of the Estremenian pig-districts is *Montanches* – mons anguis – and doubtless the hilly spot where the Duke of Arcos fed and cured 'ces petits jambons vermeils', which the Duc de St Simon ate and admired so much; 'ces jambons ont un parfum si admirable, un gout si relevé et si vivifiant, qu'on en est surpris: il est impossible de rien manger si exquis.' His grace of Arcos used to shut up the pigs in places abounding in vipers, on which they fattened. Neither the pigs, dukes, nor their toad-eaters seem to have been poisoned by these exquisite vipers . . .
>
> Be that as it may, Montanches is illustrious in pork, in which the burgesses go the whole hog, whether in the rich red sausage, the *chorizo*, or in the savoury *embuchados*, which are akin to the *mortadella* of Bologna, only less hard, and usually boiled before eating, though good also raw; they consist of the choice bits of the pig seasoned with condiments, with which, as if by redistribution, the paunch of the voracious animal is filled; the ruling passion strong in death.

Neither *jamón serrano*, which resembles Parma and Bayonne ham, but is perhaps even fuller in flavour, nor *chorizo* is cooked; both, after salting and spicing, are hung up to dry. *Jamón serrano* is best cut very thin and may be eaten on its own or with melon; *chorizo* is often served raw among the dozens of small dishes that make up Spanish *entremeses* (or *hors d'oeuvres*); it is frequently added to *cocidos* and stews of dried vegetables to lend them flavour and piquancy; it makes savoury *tortillas* (see page 166); and is also the basis for dishes such as *huevos a la flamenca* (page 25).

It is said that Charles V never let a day pass without eating Montánchez ham several times; but the last word remains with the dramatist Lope de Vega, who according to one of his early biographers, remarked:

Toda es cosa vil
a donde falta un pernil
[Life is but an empty sham
Where there is lacking Spanish ham].

Charles V, who had earlier transported wine from Valdepeñas to the ends of Europe, lost none of his love for it during his last years at Yuste. In a work published in 1667, shortly after the Emperor's death, *Amenidades, florestas y recreos de la provincia de la Vera Alta y Baja en la Extremadura*, Gabriel Acedo de la Berrueza tells of a discussion in which Charles asked a trusted German retainer which of all the places in the world he liked best. The German replied: 'The best country in the world is Spain, the best of Spain is the province of La Vera, the best of La Vera is Jarandilla, and the best place in Jarandilla is the bodega of Pedro Acedo de la Berrueza. It is therefore the best in the world, and I should like to be buried there, because its wine is the finest that exists.' When Pedro Acedo heard of this, he invited the German to his cellar to taste his wines and asked him to pick out the best. The German duly indicated two hogsheads, whereupon the generous Pedro said that one should be for his guest and the other for the Emperor. In the words of the original, 'He then went happily to the palace and told the Emperor what had transpired with the said Pedro. The Emperor, too, was pleased, and the German overjoyed when the promised consignment of wine arrived at the palace.'

Vera de Placencia still makes red wines of some repute, but like most of the wines from the Extremadura they are unobtainable outside the immediate locality. Among the best of the others are those from the small bodegas of the remote village of Salvatierra de Barros, near Zafra, south of Mérida, aromatic, brilliant and an intense ruby colour. Medellín, just east of Mérida and the birthplace of Cortés, produces wine on a larger scale, red, white and rosé, bottled under the label of 'Castillo de Medellín' and available in larger places, such as Mérida, Cáceres and Badajoz. Commercial production centres on Almendralejo in the south of the region, which, with its serried bodegas and distilleries, resembles an Extremenian Valdepeñas.

Of more interest to the wine-lover are the whites from Cañamero, on the western approach to Guadalupe, which grow a *flor* and are reminiscent of Rueda (see page 68) or the everyday drinking wine, such as Chiclana, from the sherry district. They may be sampled in the village itself or in the Parador at Guadalupe, where they are served in carafe.

Montánchez is of note, not only for its hams, but for that rarity, a red wine which grows a *flor* in the manner of sherry. It may be bought in the bars of Mérida; but if you are staying in the region, the upland village enfolded in a sierra dotted with cork oak is worth the visit to its peasant bodegas, where the wine is made in large earthenware *tinajas* (or jars), open at the top to the air. Approaching 15° in strength and somewhat turbid, it is drunk as a *chiquiteo* before meals, the white at midday and the red in the evenings, and may occasionally be found as far afield as Madrid.

Recipes

AJO BLANCO EXTREMEÑO
EXTREMENIAN GARLIC SOUP

A refreshing soup for a summer day, served ice-cold like *gazpacho*.

2 cloves garlic, peeled
Pinch of salt
2 egg yolks
3½ oz (100 g) moistened breadcrumbs
7 tablespoons olive oil
Vinegar, 1 or 2 tablespoons to taste
3½ oz (100 g) bread, diced

Either crush the garlic or grind it in a mortar with a little salt and make a smooth paste with the yolks and moistened breadcrumbs. Stir in the olive oil drop by drop as if making mayonnaise, then stir the mixture into 2½ pints (1½ litres) of cold water in a large bowl. Check the seasoning, add the vinegar and finally the diced bread. Cool well in the refrigerator before serving.

Ensalada de naranjas
Orange salad

6 oranges
3½ oz (100 g) caster sugar
3½ fl. oz (1 dl) rum

Wash, but do not peel, the oranges, then cut them into the thinnest possible rings with a sharp knife. Arrange these in a glass dish in the shape of a crown. Sprinkle with sugar, pour on a little rum (or use maraschino or kirsch), and leave for 2 to 3 hours. Serve cold.

Pure de verduras
Vegetable puree

The purée may either be served with a main dish or as a starter with croûtons of fried bread.

3 large potatoes
14 oz (400 g) tomatoes, blanched and peeled
Watercress
Salt and pepper
2 oz (60 g) butter
A pinch of sugar

Boil the potatoes, tomatoes and watercress for 20 minutes, adding a little salt and pepper. Make a purée either by rubbing the vegetables through a sieve or by putting them into a blender. Beat in the butter, add a pinch of sugar and reheat before serving.

Guisantes con jamon
Green peas with ham

Peas and green beans with chopped ham are often eaten in Spain as a starter.

4 tablespoons olive oil
1 large onion, chopped
1 large carrot, scraped and cut up
4 oz (110 g) ham or bacon, chopped
2 lb (1 kg) garden peas, shelled
Salt

Heat the olive oil in a saucepan, fry the carrot with the chopped onion until the latter turns golden, then stir in the ham. Cook for a little longer, add the peas, season with salt, then put the lid on the pan and cook very slowly until the peas are tender. Fresh peas will need about 45 minutes, and the frozen variety much less.

Patatas al estilo de Badajoz
Potatoes Badajoz style

This is in fact a hearty meat and potato pie.

2 lb (1 kg) potatoes, peeled
A little milk
3 oz (90 g) butter
Salt and pepper
2 cloves garlic
3½ oz (100 g) minced ham
3½ oz (100 g) bacon, chopped
4 fillets pork, flattened

First boil the potatoes, then mash and season them in the usual way, beating in the milk and 1 oz (30 g) of the butter.

Now crush the garlic into an oven dish and smear it over the surface. Put half of the minced ham and bacon on the bottom of the dish and dot it with half of the remaining 2 oz (60 g) of butter. Smooth the mashed potato over this and on top of the potato lay the fillets of pork. Cover with the rest of the bacon, ham and butter, sprinkle with salt and freshly-ground pepper and bake in a preheated oven (375° F/190° C/Mark 5) for ½ hour.

Coliflor al estilo de Badajoz
Cauliflower Badajoz style

An alternative to plain boiled cauliflower, often served with lamb.

1 cauliflower sufficient for 4
Salt
Chopped parsley
A little vinegar
1 egg, beaten
Flour
Olive oil

Remove the outside leaves from the cauliflower, sprinkle it with salt, parsley and vinegar, and leave for 2 hours. Now bring it to the boil in cold water, cook for 12 minutes, then drain and allow to cool. Cut it up so as to separate the branchlets, dredge them in beaten egg and flour, then fry them in hot olive oil until golden. Remove with a slotted spoon and serve hot.

Migas de pastor extremeñas
Savoury fried breadcrumbs

The Extremadura is one of the parts of Spain where you will still see the shepherd, crook in hand and leathern *bota* over his shoulder, seated under a tree or keeping slow pace with his meandering flock. At lunchtime he will quench his thirst from the *bota* and perhaps eat a *bocadillo* made from *chorizo* or cheese; in the evening the likelihood is that he will begin his meal with *migas* smoking from the pan. *Migas* are traditional peasant fare, made with variations all over the country (see also page 80); but more than that they are eaten in much grander households.

7 oz (200 g) stale bread
Salt
A little olive oil
2 cloves garlic, finely chopped
Fresh belly of pork, cut up and fried
1 chilli, deseeded and cut up

Slice the bread, put it in a bowl with water and a little salt, leave to soften for ½ hour, then remove and drain well. Heat the olive oil and the chopped garlic for 5 minutes, add the bread and stir vigorously until it is completely broken up. After 6 or 7 minutes' frying stir in the belly of pork and the chopped chilli. Cook a little longer and serve piping hot from the pan.

Tortilla extremeña
Extremenian omelette

When you are tired of more complicated fare, this omelette made from the *chorizo* so typical of the region makes a most welcome supper.

A little olive oil
½ lb (225 g) *chorizo*, skinned and thinly sliced
1 teaspoon paprika powder (sweet or hot to taste)
8 eggs, beaten
Salt
Freshly-ground white pepper

Heat a little olive oil in a large frying pan and cook the *chorizo* very briefly, adding the paprika powder. Remove with a slotted spoon and add to the beaten eggs, seasoning to taste. Using the same pan and oil, pour in the mixture. It may be cooked and folded like a French omelette or in the form of a thin pancake.

Huevos con chorizo
Eggs with chorizo

Another quickly prepared and very tasty combination of eggs and *chorizo*. Perhaps the best form of *chorizo* for this – although it does not come from the Extremadura – is the *chorizo de Pamplona*, in which the pork is finely chopped and correspondingly tender.

Olive oil
8 slices *chorizo*
8 eggs

Heat a little olive oil in a frying pan and put two of the slices of *chorizo* into it. Break an egg over each slice without delay and fry until the whites are golden and crisp at the edges. Serve at once, with slices of fried bread if you wish. Repeat the operation until all the eggs and *chorizo* have been used.

Croquetas de jamon
Ham croquettes

These croquettes, which may also be made with minced chicken, flaked fish or shrimps, may be served with a green salad as a light supper or as a starter.

2 oz (60 g) butter
2 oz (60 g) flour
17 fl. oz (½ litre) milk
7 oz (200 g) cooked ham, chopped fine
Salt
Pinch of nutmeg
1 egg, beaten
Breadcrumbs
Olive oil for frying

Melt the butter in a saucepan, add the flour, stir with a wooden spoon and pour in the milk, stirring all the time. After 5 minutes add the chopped ham, salt and nutmeg. Cook slowly for 10 minutes or until thick, then put the paste on a plate to cool.

Shape the croquettes between a couple of spoons or with your fingers if you find it easier, dredge them in beaten egg and breadcrumbs, and fry them in hot olive oil until golden.

Pollo a la Extremadura
Chicken Extremenian style

2 small chickens, each cut into 4 pieces
Olive oil
8 thin slices *jamón serrano* or ordinary ham
4 shallots, peeled
4 tomatoes, blanched, peeled and cut up
1 small glass brandy
Salt and pepper

Brown the chicken pieces in hot olive oil, drain, wrap them in the slices of ham and put them in an oven dish. Add the shallots, tomatoes and brandy, season with pepper and salt and roast in a slow oven (325° F/170° C/Mark 3) for 1 hour.

Perdices escabechadas
Preserved partridge

In the great days of the monasteries the Extremadura was well-wooded and abounded in partridge, pheasant and quail. There is still a tradition of game cookery in the region.

4 partridge (1 per person)
Olive oil
3 fl. oz (1 dl) vinegar
Freshly-ground white pepper
4 bay leaves
2 sprigs parsley
1 stick celery
4 very small onions
4 very small carrots
Salt

Truss the partridge as if for roasting, brown them in hot olive oil over a high flame, then remove them and drain the remaining oil from the saucepan. Now return the birds to the pan, adding the vinegar, freshly-ground pepper and the bay leaves, sprigs of parsley and celery, tied together as a *bouquet garni.* Cover the pan and cook gently for 10 minutes, then add the onions and carrots, together with 2½ pints (1½ litres) of water, season with salt and cook slowly for 1½ hours.

Once cooked, they may be preserved if one puts them in glass jars with the vegetables, covers them with the broth and seals them at the top with refined olive oil. Allow the liquid to cool before stoppering

the jars, and store them in a cool place. Use within three months.
To serve, cut the birds in half, surround them with the onions and carrots, arranged alternately, and pour the broth on top.

Faisan al modo de Alcantara
Pheasant Alcantara style

Among the recipes pillaged from the monastery of Alcántara by General Junot and later printed by his wife, the Duchess of Abrantes, in her *Mémoires*, was one for stuffing and roasting pheasant, which is of great historic interest in demonstrating that the monks knew of the culinary uses of truffles and duck liver centuries before they were employed in France. This recipe was reproduced in modified form by that renowned Spanish chef Ignacio Doménech in *La Nueva Cocina Elegante Española* (Madrid, 1915).

Draw the pheasant and remove the breastbone. Make the stuffing by frying duck livers in refined pork fat, seasoning with salt and pepper and rubbing through a sieve. To this purée add truffles in large pieces, previously cooked in port. Fill the cavity with this mixture and marinate the pheasant for three days in port.

Now season the bird with salt and pepper and roast it. Reduce the port wine used for the marinade, adding to it 14 to 16 small truffles. Pour this over the pheasant and simmer for 8 to 10 minutes. Serve the pheasant whole on a dish, pouring the sauce with the truffles over it, and carve it at table.

Faisanes asados
Roast pheasant

Another Estremenian recipe for cooking pheasant.

To cook

2 pheasant (large enough to cut in two)
8 rashers streaky bacon
A little butter
2 cloves garlic
Salt and pepper

To garnish

A little butter
Livers of the pheasant
1 clove garlic, squeezed
1 tablespoon cream
1 tablespoon sherry or brandy
4 slices fried bread

Wrap the pheasants in the rashers of bacon and put them in a roasting tin. Melt the butter, squeeze the garlic into it and pour over the pheasants, seasoning them with a little salt and pepper. Roast in a medium oven (350° F/180° C/Mark 4) for about ¾ hour, depending on the size.

Meanwhile melt a little butter in a frying pan, wash and dry the livers, then fry them for about 10 minutes. Drain and mince them, then add the crushed garlic, the cream, and the sherry or brandy, and stir well together with a wooden spoon. Spread the mixture on the pieces of bread, which should have been fried in olive oil until a rich golden-brown, cut the birds in half and place on top.

CALDERETA EXTREMEÑA
EXTREMENIAN LAMB HOT POT

The same recipe is often used for kid.

A little olive oil
2 cloves garlic, chopped
2 lb (1 kg) leg of lamb, boned and cut up
1 teaspoon hot paprika powder
1 bay leaf
1 wineglass dry white wine
3½ oz (100 g) lamb's liver, fried and chopped
Freshly-ground black pepper
1 or 2 canned red peppers, cut into strips
Salt
Chopped parsley

Heat some olive oil in a pan, fry the chopped garlic, then add the pieces of meat gradually and when browned transfer them to a stewpot. Once all the meat has been fried, add to it the paprika, bay leaf, white wine, chopped liver, pepper and strips of pimiento. Check the salt and if necessary add a little more wine or water and simmer gently for 1 hour or until tender. Sprinkle with chopped parsley and serve with boiled new potatoes.

FRITO EXTREMEÑO
FRIED KID EXTREMENIAN STYLE

2 lb (1 kg) leg of kid, boned and cut into large pieces
Sweet paprika powder
Olive oil
2 bay leaves
4 cloves garlic, crushed
Small glass dry white wine
Salt and pepper

Season the pieces of meat by sprinkling them with a little sweet paprika. Heat a little olive oil in a stewpot with the bay leaves, brown the pieces of meat, then add the crushed garlic, the white wine and a little salt and pepper, and cook slowly for about 1 hour until the meat is tender.

TORRIJAS CON MIEL

Torrijas are a favourite sweet in Spain, especially with children, and most regions have their own way of making and serving these golden-brown fingers.

8 slices of bread, about 1 inch (3 cm) thick
$1\frac{3}{4}$ pints (1 litre) milk
1 vanilla pod
1 cinnamon stick
4 tablespoons caster sugar
Twist of lemon peel
3 eggs, beaten
A little mixed olive oil and pork fat
A little icing sugar
1 glass Málaga or muscatelle wine
A little honey

Cut the slices of bread into fingers about 1 inch (3 cm) wide. Simmer the milk with the vanilla pod, cinnamon stick, caster sugar and lemon peel, then leave until tepid before soaking the bread in it. Leave the fingers on a plate to drain, then dredge them in the beaten egg. Meanwhile heat the mixed olive oil and pork fat in a pan, and when it is really hot fry the *torrijas* in batches until a rich golden-brown. Remove with a slotted spoon, shake on kitchen paper and sprinkle with icing sugar.

To serve, moisten them with sweet Málaga and with a little honey on top.

General Index

Abrantes, Duchess of, 6, 169
al-Andalus, 11
Albergue of Antequera, 18
Albergues, 10
Alcántara, Monastery of, 6, 159, 169
Alfonso 'the Battler', 79
Alicante, 31
alioli (*aïoli*), 2, 3, 98
almonds, 114
anchovy-fishing, 128
angulas, 129
Andalusia, 11-17
Arabic sweetmeats, 3, 18, 34, 50
Aragon, 79-83
Aragon, Crown of, 79
asparagus, Aranjuez, 49
Asturias, 142-7
Avila, 66-7

Balearic Islands, 112-6
Barcelona, 97-8
Barcelona, House of, 96
Basque Provinces, 127-30
Basques, The, 127
Bilbao, 127, 129
bocadillo, 35
bouillabaisse, 4, 33, 98, 145
buñuelo, 49
Burgos, 66
butifarra, 98, 113

Cadiz, 16, 17
cafeterías, 48
Cándido, Mesón de, 66
Carthaginians, The, 3, 7, 30, 112
Castile, New, 46-51
Castile, Old, 65-9, 142
Catalonia, 96-100
Catholic Monarchs, 8, 12, 13, 65, 79, 97, 159
cazuelas, 32
ceramics, 31
Charles V, Emperor, 4, 50, 160, 162
Chaucer, 7
Cheeses:
- Asturian, 144
- Basque, 130
- Cabrales, 144
- Galician, 144
- Mahón, 114
- Manchego, 49
- Tronchón, 32

chocolate, introduction of, 4
chocolaterías, 49
chorizo, 113, 161
churros, 49
Cid, El, 30-1, 65
cider, 144
climate, 9
coca mallorquina, 115
cochinillo, 66
Conquistadors, The, 3, 7, 30, 112
consommé, 6
Córdoba, 11
Córdoban caliphate, 4, 30, 112
Costa Brava, 97
Coto Doñana, 13

datil de mar, 34
Denominación de Origen, 83
Doménech, Ignacio, 7, 97, 169
Don Quixote, 5, 46, 48, 50
Dumas, Alexandre, 47, 49, 51, 99, 142
Drake, Sir Francis, 8

embutidos, 113

ensaimadas, 114
Escoffier, Auguste, 6, 97
Extremadura, 159-63

Ford, Richard, quoted, 1, 5, 15, 36, 51, 67, 161
Franks, The, 96
freidurías, 17

Galicia, 142-7
gazpacho, 3
Granada, 12, 17
Greeks, 30, 112
Guadalupe, Monastery of, 5, 159, 160

horchata valenciana, 36
Hosterías, 10
huertas, of Valencia, 34

James the Conqueror, 31, 97-8, 112
jamón serrano, 18, 161
Jerez de la Frontera, 13
Junot, General, 6, 169

kokotxas, 129

La Mancha, 46
Languedoc, 3, 113
lechazo, 66
lemons, introduction of, 3
Levante, 30-5
Llibre de Coch, 4, 81, 97
Lorca, García, 17

Macaulay, Rose, 30
Madrid, 47-8, 51
Maestrazgo, The, 32
Majorca, 112-6
Málaga, 12, 13, 17
Marca Hispánica, Spanish Mark, 96
María Teresa of Austria, 5
marmite, 128
Martin the Humane, 80
marzipan, 50
matanza, 113
mayonnaise, 2
'Mediterranean Tummy', 1
membrillo, 18
Mérida, 159
merienda, 49
Minorca, 113
Montánchez, 161, 162, 163
Montijo, Eugenia de, 6
Montpensier, Madame de, 5
Moors, The, 2, 7, 10, 11-12, 16, 17, 30, 65, 79, 96, 112, 128, 143, 159
morcilla, 144
Murcia, 31

Navarra, 79-83
Nola, Maestre Rubert de, 4, 81, 97

olla, 3
oranges, introduction of, 3
Oviedo, 144

paella, 33, 35
Palma de Majorca, 113
Pamplona, 75
Paradores, 10
Parador of Fuenterrabía, 33, 129
Parador del Molino Viejo, Gijón, 144
Penedès, wine museum, 99
Peninsular War, 6, 31, 143, 146, 160
Phoenicians, 16, 30, 112
phylloxera, 9, 51, 68, 116
pigeon shooting and netting, 130
pimientos, introduction of, 9
polvorones, 18
pomegranates, 114
porrón, 99
Portugal, 145
potatoes, introduction of, 4
prickly pears, 114
Provence, 3
puff pastry, 5

raisins, 34
Ramblas, The, 98
Rías of Galicia, 145
Riojano, El, 129
Romans, The, 2, 7, 50, 112, 128, 159

'Sack', 8
Salamanca, 65, 67
San Sebastián, 129
Santander, 129
Santiago de Compostela, pilgrimage to, 81, 82, 143, 159
Saragossa, 80
Sarriá, Señorío de, 81-2
Segovia, 65, 66
Seville, 11, 12, 17
sobrasada, 113
solera, 14
spices, introduction of, 2
sugar cane, introduction of, 2

tapas, 31
Tarragona, 100
Thebussem, Dr., 6, 17
tinajas, 15, 163
Toledo, 46-7, 50
tomatoes, introduction of, 4
turrón, 34-5

Unamuno, Miguel, 65

Valencia, 31, 34
venencia, 15

Wines and Spirits:
  aguardiente, 147
  Alella, 99
  anisette, 50
  Benicarló, 36
  brandy, Spanish, 50
  Cariñena, 81
  Chacolí, 130
  Chartreuse, 100
  Extremadura, 162-3
  Galicia, 8, 145-7
  Jumilla, 35
  Majorca, 115
  Málaga, 7, 8
  Montilla-Moriles, 15-16
  Navarra, 81-2
  Penedès, 99
  Perelada, 99
  qeimada, 147
  Rioja, The, 8-9, 81, 82-3
  Rueda, 68
  sangría, 100
  sherry, 7-8, 11, 13-15
  Sitges, 100
  sparkling wines, 99
  Tarragona, 8, 100
  Toro, 67
  Utiel-Requena, 35
  Valdepeñas, 48, 50, 51, 162
  Vega Sicilia, 68
  Yecla, 35
Wine terms, Spanish, 83-4

Yuste, Monastery of, 159, 160

zarzuela, 98

Index of Recipes

Adobo a la madrileña, 52
Ajo blanco extremeño, 163
Ajo blanco con uvas de Málaga, 20
Ajoharina de Jaén, 28
Albóndigas con salsa rubia, 60
Alioli, 101
Almejas de Fuenterrabía a la marinera, 134
Almond dishes:
- Almonds with pork or lamb, 94-5
- Almond soup from Ronda, 21
- Cold garlic soup with grapes, 20

Ancas de rana rebozadas, 69
Anchovy dishes:
- Salad of fresh anchovies, 132-3

Andalusian sauce, 19
Angulas en cazuela, 134
Apple dishes:
- Apple croquettes, 157
- Caramelized apple flan, 156

Aragonese sauce, 84
Arroz abanda, 40
Arroz a la marinera al estilo de Levante, 39
Arroz a la santanderina, 71
Atún o bonito a la vinagreta, 133
Atún con cebolla, 91
Atún valenciano, 42

Bacalao a la riojana, 90
Bacalao en salsa verde al estilo de Navarra, 89
Bacalao a la vizcaína, 139
Bass dishes:
- Bass with mussels or clams Asturian style, 152
- Rock bass in almond sauce, 138

Beans, broad, dishes:
- Alicante style, 37
- Asturian style, 148
- Minorcan style, 119

Beans, haricot, dishes:
- Tio Lucas, 55

Besugo al arriero, 90
Bizcocho de naranja, 44
Brains dishes:
- with black butter, 61
- with mayonnaise, 74
- Crisp fried, 61

Breadcrumbs:
- Savoury from Teruel, 88
- Savoury fried, 166

Breakfast dishes:
- Churros, 63
- Cornmeal porridge, 156

Bream:
- Sea bream country style, 90

Broad beans, *see* Beans, broad
Buñuelos de bacalao a la española, 56

Cabbage:
- Majorcan soup, 118
- Stuffed Seville style, 27

Cachelada leonesa, 72
Cakes:
- Majorcan cup, 126
- Orange, 44

Calamares a la mallorquina, 123
Calamares en su tinta, 135
Caldeirada gallega, 152-3
Caldereta de dátiles de mar, 118
Caldereta extremeña, 171
Caldillo de perro, 24-5
Callos a la madrileña, 62-3
Carne almendrada, 94-5

Cauliflower:
  Badajoz style, 165
  country style, 85
Chanfaina sauce, 108-9
Chicken dishes:
  with almonds, 59
  in Chanfaina sauce, 108-9
  in Chilindrón sauce, 92
  Extremenian style, 168
  Paella valenciana, 38-9
Chick-peas Catalan style, 109
Chilindrón sauce, 92
Chuletas de cerdo a la madrileña, 62
Chuletas de cordero a la Navarra, 94
Churros, 63
Clam dishes:
  Bass with mussels or clams Asturian style, 152
  in fish sauce, 132
  Fuenterrabía style, 134
  Quarter-of-an-hour soup, 21
Coca mallorquina, 120-1
Cochifrito, 93
Cochinillo asado, 76
Cocido castellano, 58
Cod, dried and salted:
  Bacalao Biscay style, 139
  Bacalao in green sauce Navarre style, 89
  Bacalao Rioja style, 90
  Fish croquettes, 56
  Salad from La Mancha, 53
Codornices a la casera, 72
Codornices al nido, 72-3
Coliflor al ajo arriero, 85
Coliflor al estilo de Badajoz, 165
Conejo a la asturiana, 155
Conejo a la valenciana, 43
Cordero asado al estilo de Castilla, 75
Cordero en chilindrón, 92
Costillas con alioli, 110
Crema quemada a la catalana, 111
Croquetas de jamón, 167
Croquetas de manzana, 157
Churros, 63

Desserts:
  Apple croquettes, 157
  Baked custard with brittle caramel, 111
  Caramelized apple flan, 156
  Caramelized oranges, 44
  Chestnut nougat, 45
  'Fried milk', 77
  Jam pasties, 157
  Lemon soufflé omelette, 158
  Nougat Guirlache, 44
  Nuns' delight, 95
  Peaches in red wine, 95
  Sweet omelette, 77
  Sweet pancakes, 158
  Sweet pancakes from Tarragona, 110
  A sweet from Tarragona, 110
  Tocino de cielo, 78
  Torrijas con miel, 172
Diablillos rellenos, 157
Dulces de Tarragona, 110

Eels:
  Angulas en cazuela, 134
Eggs:
  Asturian omelette, 149
  Baked eggs Navarre style, 88
  Basque omelette, 140
  Egg, cheese and bacon pie, 125
  with *chorizo*, 166
  flamenca, 25
  Majorcan style, 120
  Extremenian omelette, 166
  Lemon soufflé omelette, 158
  Majorcan egg and vegetable pie, 119
  Omelette Sacromonte, 26
  Revoltillo de sobrasada, 124
  Sardine omelette, 122
  Spanish omelette, 56-7
Empanada gallega, 154
Empanadillas valencianas, 42
Ensalada de boquerones, 132-3
Ensalada levantina, 36
Ensalada manchega, 52
Ensalada de naranjas, 164
Ensalada sevillana, 22

Faisán al modo de Alcántara, 169
Faisanes asados, 170
Farines o farrapes, 156
Faves al Tombet, 37
Filloas, 158
Fish dishes:
  Anchovy salad, 132-3
  Angulas en cazuela, 134
  Arroz abanda, 40
  Bacalao Biscay style, 139
  Bacalao in green sauce Navarre style, 89
  Bacalao Rioja style, 90

Basque-style hake, 136
Bass with mussels or clams Asturian style, 152
Caldereta de dátiles de mar, 118
Caldillo de perro, 24-5
Catalan mussel soup, 103
Clams in fish sauce, 132
Clams Fuenterrabía style, 134
Crisp-fried prawns in batter, 138-9
Fish croquettes, 56
Fish sauce, 132
Fish soup, 102
Fried prawns, 23
Galician fish stew, 152-3
Hake Galician style, 150
Hake with mayonnaise and tomato sauce, 136-7
Inkfish in their own ink, 135
Kokotxas de merluza, 137
Lobster Catalan style, 106-7
Lobster Majorcan style, 122
Marinated fish, 70
Mixed fried fish Andalusian style, 24
Mixed grilled fish with Romesco sauce, 104
Paella marinera, 38, 140
Potato sauce for fish, 22
Prawns with chillies, 149
Rice with fish Levante style, 39
Rock bass in almond sauce, 138
A salad from La Mancha, 53
Sardine omelette, 122
Sardines Asturian style, 151
Scallops Galician style, 150
Stuffed inkfish Majorcan style, 123
Sardines in tomato sauce, 41
Sea bream country style, 90
Tuna with onion, 91
Tuna fish Valencian style, 42
Tuna with vinaigrette sauce, 133
Valencian fish pasties, 42-3
Vinaigrette sauce for fish, 101
Zarzuela de mariscos, 106

Flan de manzanas, 156
Forcemeat for *cocidos*, 59
Frito extremeño, 171
Fritos variados de pescados a la andaluza, 24
Frogs' legs, fried, 69

Gambas fritas, 23
Gambas al pil pil, 149
Gambas rebozadas, 138-9
Garbanzos a la catalana, 109
Garbure, 85
Garlic dishes:
Cold garlic soup with grapes, 20
sauce, 101
soup with eggs, 54
Extremenian garlic soup, 163
Gazpacho andaluz, 19
Gazpacho caliente gaditano, 20
Goat, *see* Kid
Greixera mallorquina, 125
Guisantes con jamón, 164

Habas a la asturiana, 148
Habas al estilo de Mahón, 119
Hake:
Basque-style, 136
Galician style, 150
with mayonnaise and tomato sauce, 136-7
Kokotxas de merluza, 137
Ham:
Green peas with, 164
croquettes, 167
Savoury tart from Galicia, 154
Haricot beans, *see* Beans, haricot
Hazelnut soup, 148
Huevos con chorizo, 167
Huevos a la flamenca, 25
Huevos a la mallorquina, 120
Huevos al plato a la Navarre, 88

Inkfish:
in their own ink, 135
Mixed fried fish Andalusian style, 24
Paella marinera, 140
Paella valenciana, 38
Stuffed Majorcan style, 123

Judías al Tío Lucas, 55

Kid:
Extremenian hot pot, 171
Fried Extremenian style, 171
Roast leg of, 75
Kidneys in sherry, 28
Kokotxas de merluza, 136

Lamb dishes:
Cochifrito, 93
Extremenian hot pot, 171
chops Navarre style, 94
in Chilindrón sauce, 92

Roast Castilian style, 75
Roast Aragonese style, 93
Roast leg of, 75
Langosta a la catalana, 106-7
Langosta a la mallorquina, 122
Leche frita, 77
Lentejas zamoranas, 70
Lentils Zamora style, 70
Liadillos sevillanos, 27
Lobster dishes:
Catalan style, 106-7
Majorcan style, 122
Lomo de cerdo al estilo vasco, 141
Lomo a la mallorquina, 125
Lubina a la asturiana, 152

Manjar de monjas, 95
Marinades:
for fish, 70
for pork, 52
Mayonnaise, 116-17
Andalusian sauce, 19
Mazapanes de Toledo, 64
Meatballs:
Catalan soup with, 104
in sauce, 60
Mejillones con salsa marinera, 132
Melocotones con vino tinto, 95
Menestra de Tudela, 86
Merluza a la gallega, 150
Merluza con mahonesa y salsa de tomate, 136-7
Merluza a la vasca, 136
Mero en salsa de almendras, 138
Migas al estilo de Teruel, 88
Migas de pastor extremeñas, 166
Mushrooms Maestrazgo style, 37
Mussels:
Bass with mussels or clams Asturian style, 152
Caldereta de dátiles de mar, 118
Catalan soup, 103
Paella marinera, 38, 140

Naranjas acarameladas, 44
Nougat, 44-5

Offal:
Kidneys in sherry, 28
Omelette Sacromonte, 26
Olive sauce, 131
Omelettes:
Asturian, 149
Basque, 140
Extremenian, 166
Lemon soufflé, 158
Sacromonte, 26
Sardine, 122
Spanish, 56-7
Sweet, 77
Oranges:
Caramelized, 44
Salad, 164
Orelletas de Tarragona, 110

Paella marinera, 38, 140
Paella valenciana, 38-9
Pancakes:
Sweet, 158
Sweet from Tarragona, 110
Parrillada de pescado con salsa romesco, 104
Partridge:
Bullfighter's, 26-7
Catalan style, 108
Preserved, 168
Stewed, 74
Stewed with chocolate, 73
Pastelitos mallorquines, 126
Pastry:
Churros, 63
Pestiños madrileños, 64
Patatas castellanas, 55
Patatas al estilo de Badajoz, 165
Peaches in red wine, 95
Peas, chick-, *see* Chick-peas
Peas, green, with ham, 164
Pepitoria de gallina, 59
Peppers, stuffed, Rioja style, 87
Perdices de capellán, 124
Perdices escabechadas, 168
Perdices estofadas, 74
Perdices estofadas con chocolate, 73
Perdices a la torera, 26-7
Perdiz a la catalana, 108
Pescado a medio escabeche, 70
Pestiños madrileños, 64
Pheasant:
Alcántara style, 169
Roast, 170
Pierna de cabrito asada, 75
Pies:
Coca mallorquina, 120-1
Egg, cheese and bacon, 125
Majorcan egg and vegetable, 119
Potatoes Badajoz style, 165
Savoury tart from Galicia, 154
Pimientos rellenos a la riojana, 87

Piperada vasca, 140
Pisto castellano, 71
Pollo en chanfaina, 108-9
Pollo a la chilindrón, 92
Pollo a la Extremadura, 168
Polvorones sevillanos, 29
Pork:
  Loin of, Basque style, 141
  Loin of, Majorcan style, 125
  Marinade for, 52
  with almonds, 94
  chops Madrid style, 62
  Potatoes Badajoz style, 165
  Ribs of with alioli sauce, 110
  Roast sucking pig, 76
  Stuffed peppers Rioja style, 87
Porridge, cornmeal, 156
Potatoes:
  Badajoz style, 165
  Castilian style, 55
  sauce for fish, 22
  with spiced sausage, 72
  Spiced from Jaén, 28
  Spanish omelette, 56
Prawns:
  Crisp-fried in batter, 138-9
  Fried, 23
  with chillis, 149
Puré de verduras, 164

Quail:
  country style, 72
  in nest, 72-3

Rabbit:
  in cider Asturian style, 155
  Valencian style, 43
Revoltillo de sobrasada, 124
Rice:
  Arroz abanda, 40
  Paella valenciana, 38
  with fish Levante style, 39
  Santander style, 71
Riñones al Jerez, 28
Robellones al estilo del Maestrazgo, 37
Romesco sauce, 105

Salads:
  Orange, 164
  fresh anchovy, 132-3
  La Mancha, 52
  Levante, 36
  Seville, 22
Salsa de aceitunas, 131
Salsa a la andaluza, 19
Salsa aragonesa, 84
Salsa española, 51
Salsa mahonesa, 116-17
Salsa mahonesa verde, 117
Salsa a la marinera, 132
Salsa de patata para pescado, 22
Salsa rubia, 60
Salsa tártara, 117
Salsa vinagreta para pescados cocidos, 101
Salsa al vino blanco, 131
Sardinas a la asturiana, 151
Sardinas al estilo de Cartagena, 41
Sauces:
  Andalusian, 19
  Aragonese, 84
  Chanfaina, 108-9
  Chilindrón, 92
  Garlic, 101
  Green mayonnaise, 118
  Mayonnaise, 116-17
  Olive, 131
  Potato for fish, 22
  Romesco, 105
  Salsa española, 51
  Salsa rubia, 60
  Tartare, 117
  Tomato, 41
  Vinaigrette, 22
  Vinaigrette, for fish, 101
  White wine, 131
Sausage:
  Baked eggs Navarre style, 88
  Broad beans Minorcan style, 119
  Chaplain's 'Partridge', 124
  Chick-peas Catalan style, 109
  Eggs Majorcan style, 120
  Eggs with *chorizo*, 167
  Loin of pork Majorcan style, 125
  Potatoes with spiced, 72
  Revoltillo de sobrasada, 124
  Savoury tart from Galicia, 154
Scallops Galician style, 150
Sesos bandera española, 74
Sesos empanados, 61
Sesos a la manteca negra, 61
Sopa de ajo con huevos, 53
Sopa de albóndiguillas catalana, 104
Sopa de almendras de Ronda, 21
Sopa de avellanas, 148
Sopa al cuarto de hora, 21
Sopa mallorquina, 118

Sopa de mejillones catalana, 103
Sopa de pescado, 102
Sopa toledana, 54
Soups, cold:
  Cold garlic, with grapes, 20
  Gazpacho Andalusian style, 19
Soups, hot:
  Almond from Ronda, 21
  Caldereta de dátiles de mar, 118
  Caldillo de perro, 24-5
  Catalan mussel, 103
  Catalan with meat balls, 104
  Extremenian garlic, 163
  Fish, 102
  Garlic, with eggs, 53
  Hot gazpacho from Cadiz, 20
  Hazelnut, 148
  Majorcan, 118
  Quarter-of-an-hour, 21
  Toledan, 54
  Vegetable, from Navarra, 85
Squid, *see* Inkfish
Starters:
  Ajoharina de Jaén, 28
  Brains with mayonnaise, 74
  Green peas with ham, 164
  Haricot beans Tío Lucas, 55
  Marinated fish, 70
  Mixed vegetable dish from Tudela, 86
  Pisto castellano, 71
  Potatoes Castilian style, 55
  Prawns with chillis, 149
  Salad from La Mancha, 53
  Savoury breadcrumbs from Teruel, 88
  Vegetable purée, 164
Stews:
  Bullfighter's partridge, 26-7
  Cochifrito, 93
  Cocido castellano, 58
  Extremenian lamb hot pot, 171
  Fried kid Extremenian style, 171
  Galician fish stew, 152-3
  Lentils Zamora style, 70
  Rabbit in cider Asturian style, 155
  Zarzuela de mariscos, 106
Stuffing, traditional, for sucking pig, 76
Sucking-pig, roast, 76
Supper dishes:
  Basque omelette, 140
  Eggs Majorcan style, 120
  Mixed vegetable dish from Tudela, 86
  Rice Santander style, 71
Sweetmeats:
  Marzipan, 64
  Nougat Guirlache, 44
  Polvorones sevillanos, 29
  Yolks of Santa Teresa, 78
Tartare sauce, 117
Tarts, *see* Pies
Ternasco asado, 93
Tocino de cielo, 78
Tomato sauce, 41
Torrijas con miel, 172
Tortilla a la asturiana, 149
Tortilla azucarada, 77
Tortilla extremeña, 166
Tortilla de patatas a la española, 56-7
Tortilla al Sacromonte, 26
Tortilla de sardinas frescas, 122
Tortilla soplada al limón, 158
Tripe Madrid style, 62-3
Tumbet, 119
Tuna:
  with onion, 91
  Valencia style, 42
  with vinaigrette sauce, 133
Turrón de castañas, 45
Turrón de Guirlache, 44

Veal:
  Chaplain's 'partridge', 124
Vegetables:
  Broad beans Alicante style, 37
  Broad beans Asturian style, 148
  Broad beans Minorcan style, 119
  Cauliflower Badajoz style, 165
  Cauliflower country style, 85
  Mixed vegetable dish from Tudela, 86
  Mushrooms Maestrazgo style, 37
  Pisto castellano, 71
  Potatoes Castilian style, 55
  Spiced potatoes from Jaén, 28
  Vegetable purée, 164
  Vegetable relish, 41
Vieiras gallegas, 150
Vinaigrette sauce, 22, 101

White wine sauce, 131
Whiting:
  Caldillo de perro, 25

Yemas de Santa Teresa, 78

Zarzuela de marisco, 106